INTO THE MILLE

ANGLO-BOER WAR
Centenary Diary

TODAY AND 100 YEARS AGO

QUOTES FROM THE PAST: VISIONS OF THE FUTURE

OCTOBER1899 – DECEMBER 1900
OCTOBER1999 – DECEMBER 2000

FOCUS ON LADYSMITH: 'THE EYE OF THE WAR' AND NATAL: 'THE MOST CRUCIAL FRONT'

COMPILED BY
MAUREEN RICHARDS
ALIAS 'THE SIEGETOWN LYRE'

It is a good thing for an uneducated man to read books of quotations.
WSCH

A lamentable tale of things done long ago - and ill-done.
DR

Shuter & Shooter
PIETERMARITZBURG • CAPETOWN • RANDBURG

I need to deeply thank a dear friend and mentor, Dr Bernard Kemp; my three children, Lynton, Michael and Melanie; my father, Stan Davies; my two brothers Norman and Mel and thus Liz and Michelle; Maureen and Keith Jones, Frikkie Richards, Nic Ruddiman and Thomas Story.

Without their unfailing support, their belief in my ability, and their encouragement, this work would not have been completed.

My thanks also to those at Shuters for their friendship, round the clock effort and dedication to bring about this once in a thousand years publication.

Shuter & Shooter (Pty) Ltd
Gray's Inn, 230 Church Street
Pietermaritzburg, South Africa 3201

First edition 1999

ISBN 0 7960 1493 0

Printed by The Natal Witness
Printing and Publishing Company (Pty) Ltd
Pietermaritzburg
7341

The Siegetown Lyre

As seen on BBC1: Time Watch: 18.3.97

The Boer War: the First Media War

Maureen Richards: Teller of Tall Stories

Curator: Ladysmith Siege Museum 1987-1995
Satour: Military History Specialist Tourist Guide 1987

> *How shall I find space to tell half of the incidents?*
>
> *Bennet Burleigh 1899*

> *And do not be so hard, next time, please, on the poor Sir Redvers. Splendid chap. And a good sport, indeed.*

1 May 1999 ... After a tour of the Relief Battles:

I wish to thank you for the copies of the history of the inner court manoeuvres not performed on the public stage. I find rather amusing how histories, regardless of the setting, time, personalities, circumstances, always fit some general pattern.

I found your presentation most charming, the point of your sense of humour (or which of it I was capable to comprehend) giving it the most desirable dimension. I felt almost from the start that if you could enjoy a totally unrestricted freedom the trip could turn into one continuous stream of hilarity. To fully appreciate it all, I will always come short (not being by nature an ardent insider for really anything) but when I will reread the Boer War history, there will be definitely a Natal chapter written by you.

For this I am most grateful.

B Libicek

The South African War: 1899-1902

The Boer War was other than most wars. It was a vast tragedy in the life of a people, whose human interest far surpassed its military value: an epic struggle between the smallest and the greatest of peoples.

Wars pass, but the human soul endures; the interest not so much in the war as in the human experience behind it.

Jan Smuts

DEDICATED WITH LOVE TO MY MOTHER

'I THANK MY GOD IN ALL MY REMEMBRANCE OF YOU.'

PHILIPPIANS 1:3

'LET THE MEASURE OF ITS TRUTH BE THE MEASURE OF ITS USEFULNESS.' – JPF

Personal information

Name: ....

Address: ....

....

Telephone No: (H) .... (W) ....

Cellular phone: ....

E-mail: ....

Identification No: ....

In case of emergency, contact:

Name: ....

Telephone No: (H) .... (W) ....

Cellular phone: ....

Address: ....

Acknowledgements

Concept and sources of quotations:

The War happened one hundred years ago – every effort has thus been made to quote from sources of the time. As the media featured so prominently, so did the host of newspaper correspondents at the turn of the century: John Black Atkins of the *Manchester Guardian;* George Warrington Steevens of the *Daily Mail;* Bennet Burleigh of the *Daily Telegraph;* Henry Nevinson of the *Daily Chronicle;* Winston Spencer Churchill of the *Morning Post;* and the master himself, Leo Amery of the *Times.* Dr Arthur Conan Doyle who penned *The Great Boer War,* and W. H. Wilson's two volumes *With the Flag to Pretoria* add to the variety of sources. *With the Flag* provides wonderful illustrative material and biographical details in respect of the leading personalities, both Boer and Briton alike. Postcards illustrated by Dutch and French artists, aptly adapted, make light of the very seriousness of the war and the reasons for it. This England's *Register of the Victoria Cross* is an invaluable source of extensively researched facts, complemented by John Percival's *For Valour.* W. K-L. Dickson and his *Biograph in Battle* could not be ignored for his keen and carefully recorded descriptions of operations particularly on the Colenso Front.

Having concentrated my field of research, to a large extent, on the Churchills, from the many books in my collection, Brian Roberts takes some beating in his carefully researched *Churchills in Africa,* comprehensively including so many facets of their individual experiences in South Africa before and at the turn of the century. Brian Roberts is thus the only contemporary author fairly extensively quoted. Others, quoted less frequently, are included in the bibliography on the following page.

INVASION: 'A WHOLE ARMY CORPS WOULD SCARCELY HAVE SUFFICED TO BAR ALL THOSE DOORS INTO NATAL. THE PRACTICAL QUESTION WAS NOT WHETHER ALL NATAL SHOULD BE INVADED, BUT HOW MUCH SHOULD BE ABANDONED!' – JBA

Bibliography

Copyright material

Every effort has been made to identify the holders of copyright to material used in this book.
The publishers apologise for any errors or omissions, and would be grateful for information enabling them to correct these.

The compiler acknowledges using quotations and/or photographs and illustrations from the following publications:

The Relief of Ladysmith: John Black Atkins – Methuen & Co, 36 Essex Street, London (1900)

From Cape Town to Ladysmith: George Warrington Steevens – William Blackwood & Sons, London (1900)

Natal Campaign: Bennet Burleigh – George Bell & Sons, London (1900)

Ladysmith: The Diary of a Siege: Henry Nevinson – Methuen & Co, 36 Essex Street, London (1900)

London to Ladysmith: Winston Spencer Churchill – Longmans, Green & Co, 39 Paternoster Row, London (1900)

The Times History of the War in South Africa: Leo Amery – Sampson Low, Marston & Co Ltd, London (1909)

The Great Boer War: Arthur Conan Doyle – Smith, Elder & Co, London (1900)

With the Flag to Pretoria: W. H. Wilson – The Amalgamated Press Ltd, London (1902)

The Biograph in Battle: W. K-L. Dickson – T. Fisher Unwin, Paternoster Square, London (1901)

De Boerenoorlog in Oude Ansichten: H. J. de Graaf – Europese Biblioteek-Zaltbommel, Nederland (1922)

The Siege of Ladysmith: Gerald Sharp – Macdonald & Jane's Publishers Ltd, London (1976)

The Jameson Raid: Elizabeth Longford – Jonathan Ball Publishers, Johannesburg (1982)

The Life of General Sir Charles Warren: Watkin Williams – Basil Blackwell, Oxford, UK (1941)

The Battle of Spion Kop: Oliver Ransford – John Murray, Albemarle Street, London (1960)

The Story of the Imperial Light Horse: G. F. Gibson – G. D. & Co, Johannesburg (1937)

President Paul Kruger: Johannes Meintjies – Cassell & Collier Macmillan Publishers Ltd, 35 Red Square, London (1974)

Three Years War: Christiaan De Wet – Archibald Constable & Co Ltd, London (1902)

A Churchill Family Album: Mary Soames – Book Club Associates, London (1982)

The Transvaal from Within: J. P. FitzPatrick – William Heinemann, London (1899)

Fitz: J. P. R. Wallis – Macmillan & Co Ltd, London (1955)

The First South African: A. P. Cartwright – Purnell & Sons (SA) (Pty) Ltd, 70 Keerom Street, Cape Town (1971)

The Life of Lord Roberts: David James – Hollis & Carter, London (1954)

Listening for the Drums: Ian Hamilton – Faber & Faber Ltd, 24 Russell Square, London (1944)

Commando: Deneys Reitz – Praeger Publishers Inc., Fourth Ave, New York (1970)

For Valour: John Percival – Methuen Ltd, 11 Fetter Lane, London (1986)

South Africa and the Transvaal War: Louis Creswick – The Caxton Publishing Co, London (1901)

Ons Eerste Ses Premiers: Piet Meiring – Publisher's details unknown

Special Double Number: The Graphic – Illustrated London News & Sketch Ltd, 198 Strand, London (1900)

Diary No. 6: Kate Driver, Ladysmith Historical Society, Ladysmith

The Royal Tournament: 1994 Programme – Wellington Barracks, London (1994)

Archival Material from the Ladysmith Siege Museum

The Selected Works of Mahatma Gandhi: M. K. Gandhi – Publisher's details unknown

Aldershot Review: John Walters – Publisher's details unknown

The Ladysmith Siege: G. W. Lines – Town Clerk, Ladysmith (1900)

Battles of the Boer War: W. Baring Pemberton – BT Babford Ltd, 4 Fitzharding Street, Portman Square, London (1964)

Churchills in Africa: Brian Roberts – Hamish Hamilton Ltd, 90 Great Russell Street, London (1970)

Campaigns of a War Correspondent: Melton Prior – Publisher's details unknown

Buller's Campaign: Julian Symons – The Great Press, 11 Fitzroy Square, London (1963)

All 63 citations for VCs awarded in the Anglo-Boer War are taken from
The Register of the Victoria Cross
with the kind permission of the publishers – This England, Alma House, Rodney Road, Cheltenham, Glos. GL50 1HT.

1899

JANUARY

S	M	T	W	T	F	S
1	2	3	4	5	6	7
8	9	10	11	12	13	14
15	16	17	18	19	20	21
22	23	24	25	26	27	28
29	30	31				

FEBRUARY

S	M	T	W	T	F	S
			1	2	3	4
5	6	7	8	9	10	11
12	13	14	15	16	17	18
19	20	21	22	23	24	25
26	27	28				

MARCH

S	M	T	W	T	F	S
			1	2	3	4
5	6	7	8	9	10	11
12	13	14	15	16	17	18
19	20	21	22	23	24	25
26	27	28	29	30	31	

APRIL

S	M	T	W	T	F	S
						1
2	3	4	5	6	7	8
9	10	11	12	13	14	15
16	17	18	19	20	21	22
23/30	24	25	26	27	28	29

MAY

S	M	T	W	T	F	S
	1	2	3	4	5	6
7	8	9	10	11	12	13
14	15	16	17	18	19	20
21	22	23	24	25	26	27
28	29	30	31			

JUNE

S	M	T	W	T	F	S
				1	2	3
4	5	6	7	8	9	10
11	12	13	14	15	16	17
18	19	20	21	22	23	24
25	26	27	28	29	30	

JULY

S	M	T	W	T	F	S
						1
2	3	4	5	6	7	8
9	10	11	12	13	14	15
16	17	18	19	20	21	22
23/30	24/31	25	26	27	28	29

AUGUST

S	M	T	W	T	F	S
		1	2	3	4	5
6	7	8	9	10	11	12
13	14	15	16	17	18	19
20	21	22	23	24	25	26
27	28	29	30	31		

SEPTEMBER

S	M	T	W	T	F	S
					1	2
3	4	5	6	7	8	9
10	11	12	13	14	15	16
17	18	19	20	21	22	23
24	25	26	27	28	29	30

OCTOBER

S	M	T	W	T	F	S
1	2	3	4	5	6	7
8	9	10	11	12	13	14
15	16	17	18	19	20	21
22	23	24	25	26	27	28
29	30	31				

NOVEMBER

S	M	T	W	T	F	S
			1	2	3	4
5	6	7	8	9	10	11
12	13	14	15	16	17	18
19	20	21	22	23	24	25
26	27	28	29	30	31	

DECEMBER

S	M	T	W	T	F	S
					1	2
3	4	5	6	7	8	9
10	11	12	13	14	15	16
17	18	19	20	21	22	23
24/31	25	26	27	28	29	30

1900

JANUARY

S	M	T	W	T	F	S
	1	2	3	4	5	6
7	8	9	10	11	12	13
14	15	16	17	18	19	20
21	22	23	24	25	26	27
28	29	30	31			

FEBRUARY

S	M	T	W	T	F	S
				1	2	3
4	5	6	7	8	9	10
11	12	13	14	15	16	17
18	19	20	21	22	23	24
25	26	27	28			

MARCH

S	M	T	W	T	F	S
				1	2	3
4	5	6	7	8	9	10
11	12	13	14	15	16	17
18	19	20	21	22	23	24
25	26	27	28	29	30	31

APRIL

S	M	T	W	T	F	S
1	2	3	4	5	6	7
8	9	10	11	12	13	14
15	16	17	18	19	20	21
22	23	24	25	26	27	28
29	30					

MAY

S	M	T	W	T	F	S
		1	2	3	4	5
6	7	8	9	10	11	12
13	14	15	16	17	18	19
20	21	22	23	24	25	26
27	28	29	30	31		

JUNE

S	M	T	W	T	F	S
					1	2
3	4	5	6	7	8	9
10	11	12	13	14	15	16
17	18	19	20	21	22	23
24	25	26	27	28	29	30

JULY

S	M	T	W	T	F	S
1	2	3	4	5	6	7
8	9	10	11	12	13	14
15	16	17	18	19	20	21
22	23	24	25	26	27	28
29	30	31				

AUGUST

S	M	T	W	T	F	S
			1	2	3	4
5	6	7	8	9	10	11
12	13	14	15	16	17	18
19	20	21	22	23	24	25
26	27	28	29	30	31	

SEPTEMBER

S	M	T	W	T	F	S
						1
2	3	4	5	6	7	8
9	10	11	12	13	14	15
16	17	18	19	20	21	22
23/30	24	25	26	27	28	29

OCTOBER

S	M	T	W	T	F	S
	1	2	3	4	5	6
7	8	9	10	11	12	13
14	15	16	17	18	19	20
21	22	23	24	25	26	27
28	29	30	31			

NOVEMBER

S	M	T	W	T	F	S
				1	2	3
4	5	6	7	8	9	10
11	12	13	14	15	16	17
18	19	20	21	22	23	24
25	26	27	28	29	30	

DECEMBER

S	M	T	W	T	F	S
						1
2	3	4	5	6	7	8
9	10	11	12	13	14	15
16	17	18	19	20	21	22
23/30	24/31	25	26	27	28	29

1999

OCTOBER

S	M	T	W	T	F	S
					1	2
3	4	5	6	7	8	9
10	11	12	13	14	15	16
17	18	19	20	21	22	23
24/31	25	26	27	28	29	30

NOVEMBER

S	M	T	W	T	F	S
	1	2	3	4	5	6
7	8	9	10	11	12	13
14	15	16	17	18	19	20
21	22	23	24	25	26	27
28	29	30				

DECEMBER

S	M	T	W	T	F	S
			1	2	3	4
5	6	7	8	9	10	11
12	13	14	15	16	17	18
19	20	21	22	23	24	25
26	27	28	29	30	31	

2000

JANUARY

S	M	T	W	T	F	S
						1
2	3	4	5	6	7	8
9	10	11	12	13	14	15
16	17	18	19	20	21	22
23/30	24/31	25	26	27	28	29

FEBRUARY

S	M	T	W	T	F	S
		1	2	3	4	5
6	7	8	9	10	11	12
13	14	15	16	17	18	19
20	21	22	23	24	25	26
27	28	29				

MARCH

S	M	T	W	T	F	S
			1	2	3	4
5	6	7	8	9	10	11
12	13	14	15	16	17	18
19	20	21	22	23	24	25
26	27	28	29	30	31	

APRIL

S	M	T	W	T	F	S
						1
2	3	4	5	6	7	8
9	10	11	12	13	14	15
16	17	18	19	20	21	22
23/30	24	25	26	27	28	29

MAY

S	M	T	W	T	F	S
	1	2	3	4	5	6
7	8	9	10	11	12	13
14	15	16	17	18	19	20
21	22	23	24	25	26	27
28	29	30	31			

JUNE

S	M	T	W	T	F	S
				1	2	3
4	5	6	7	8	9	10
11	12	13	14	15	16	17
18	19	20	21	22	23	24
25	26	27	28	29	30	

JULY

S	M	T	W	T	F	S
						1
2	3	4	5	6	7	8
9	10	11	12	13	14	15
16	17	18	19	20	21	22
23/30	24/31	25	26	27	28	29

AUGUST

S	M	T	W	T	F	S
		1	2	3	4	5
6	7	8	9	10	11	12
13	14	15	16	17	18	19
20	21	22	23	24	25	26
27	28	29	30	31		

SEPTEMBER

S	M	T	W	T	F	S
					1	2
3	4	5	6	7	8	9
10	11	12	13	14	15	16
17	18	19	20	21	22	23
24	25	26	27	28	29	30

OCTOBER

S	M	T	W	T	F	S
1	2	3	4	5	6	7
8	9	10	11	12	13	14
15	16	17	18	19	20	21
22	23	24	25	26	27	28
29	30					

NOVEMBER

S	M	T	W	T	F	S
			1	2	3	4
5	6	7	8	9	10	11
12	13	14	15	16	17	18
19	20	21	22	23	24	25
26	27	28	29	30		

DECEMBER

S	M	T	W	T	F	S
					1	2
3	4	5	6	7	8	9
10	11	12	13	14	15	16
17	18	19	20	21	22	23
24/31	25	26	27	28	29	30

The Royal Navy Field Gun Competition

The Royal Navy Field Gun Competition originates from the South African War when, in 1899, guns from HMS Ships *Terrible* and *Powerful* were taken ashore and transported hundreds of miles across land before going into action. The competition in its present form was first run at the Royal Tournament in 1907.

Three teams representing the naval commands of Portsmouth, Devonport and the Fleet Air Arm compete against each other for the duration of the Royal Tournament in a fiercely contested fight for four important trophies.

South Africa 1899

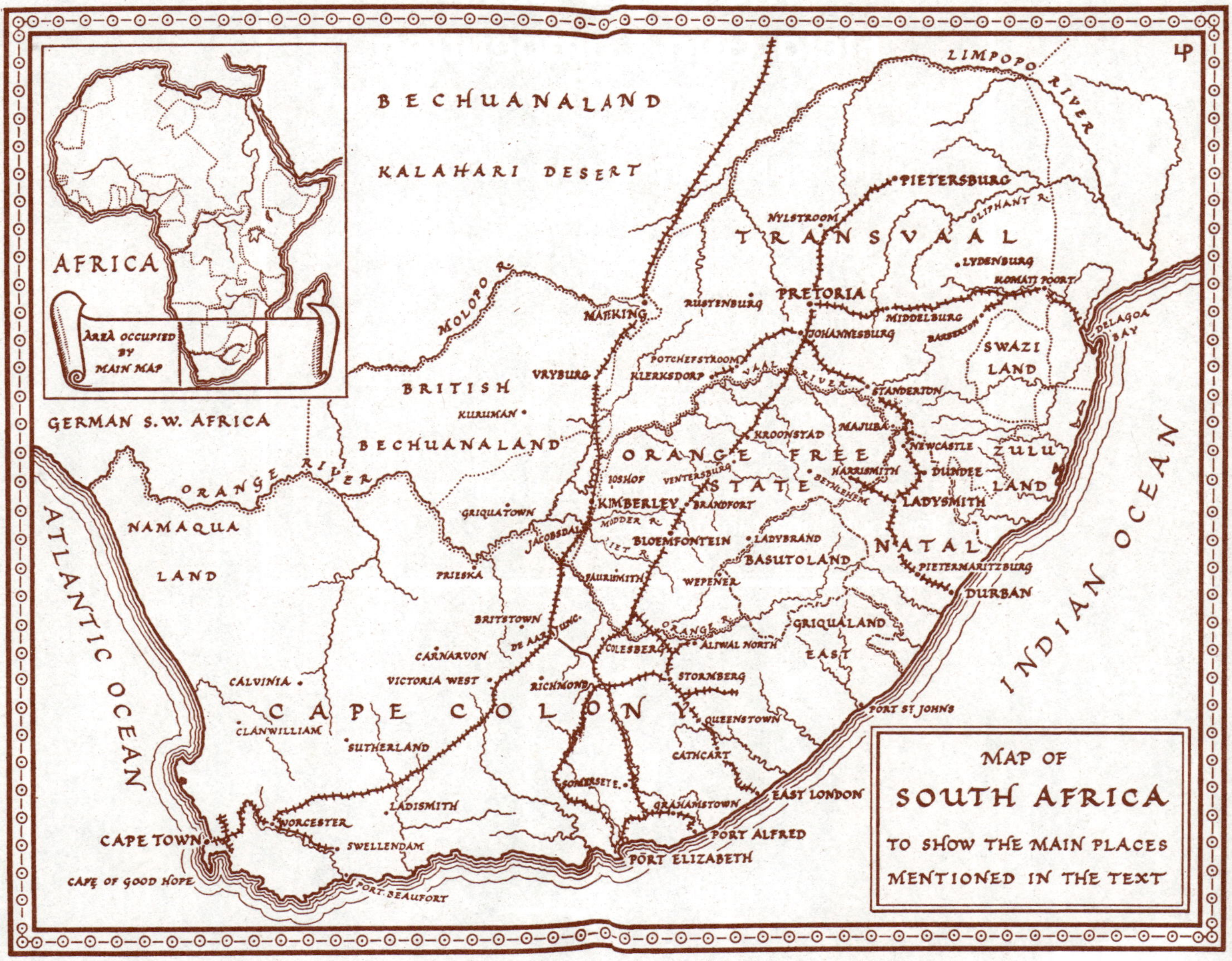

Boer vs Brit : Fighting Country

The fighting is always bound to be hard, because we stand at a certain natural disadvantage. One has only to look round at the frequent kopjes covered with boulders and crevices which afford shelter to the trained or the cunning to say:

'This is Boers' fighting country, not ours.'

This natural disadvantage, since we were not born or trained to the country, we cannot hope to overcome. The British officer, with the manuals of tactics at his finger ends, is constantly finding himself in predicaments of which the manuals offer no solution; and however clever he be, his men are hard to extricate from their position, for their sturdy discipline is matched with an equally sturdy want of natural resource, intelligence, or eye for the country. The Boer knows the common features of the country like the palm of his hand; while British troops are mobilizing, he is, as it were, deer-stalking; the British officer leads a difficult movement prescribed for rare occasions, the Boer meets it by saying 'Come on Piet'. It is astonishing to us that the irregular should be in any respect superior to the regular, but is not this a new thing which armies of Europe must allow in their calculation? This natural advantage of the Boer belongs to him only in the country of the kopjes or in very broken ground. In fair open country where British cavalry perform their proper functions the results would certainly be different.

Natal Colony Map

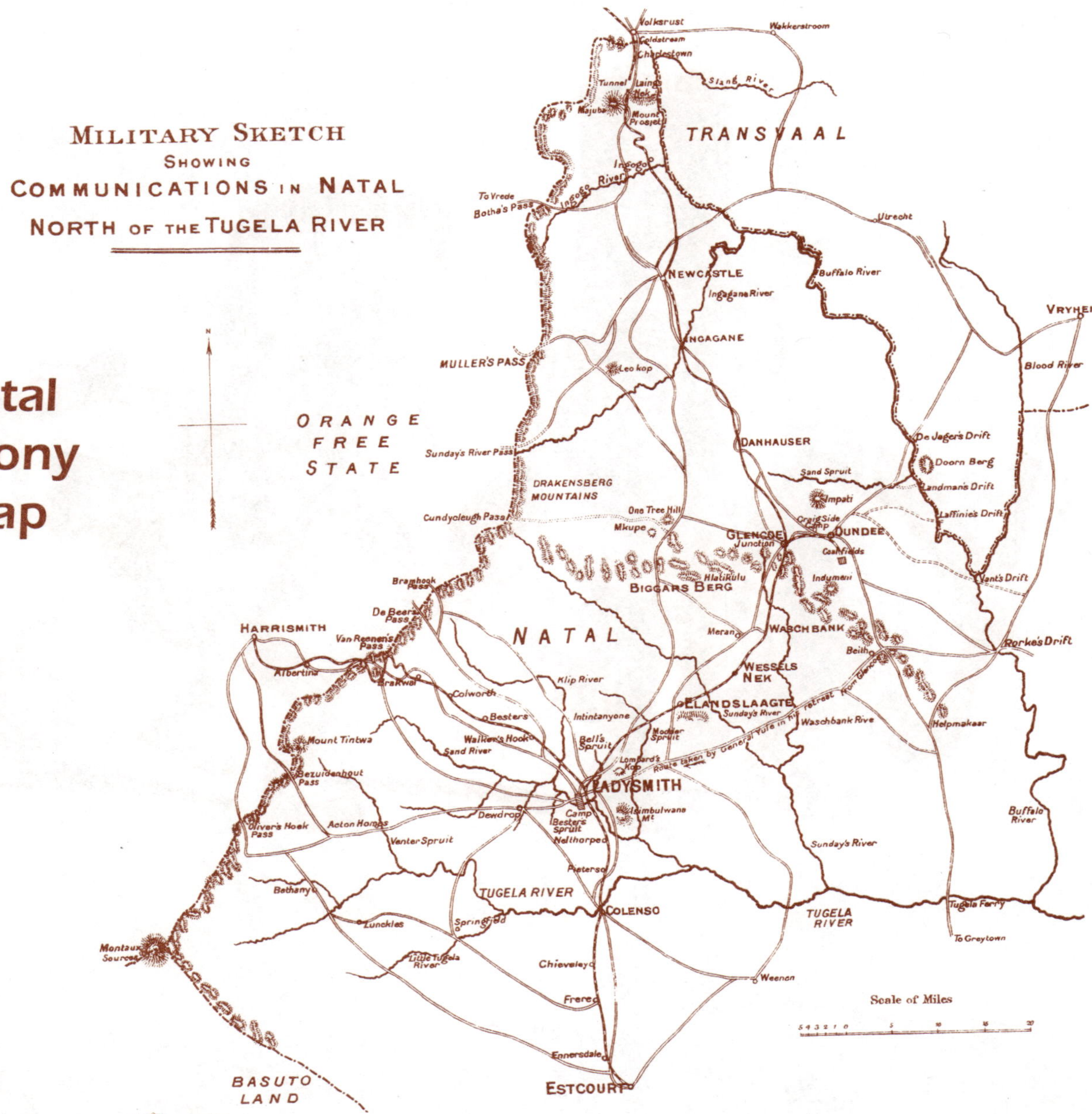

It is easy now to read the warnings of the map. A better field than Natal for the operations of the allies could not have been designed. No other British colony has two frontiers, one with the Transvaal and another with the Orange Free State, nowhere else could the allies, advancing from his own base, combine in a simultaneous forward movement. The ground, moreover, suits Boer tactics, and the very shape of the frontiers, which already north of the Tugela seemed to yield and contract under growing pressure from either flank, plainly invited those enveloping movements, which are the beginning and end of Boer strategy. Indeed, had the allies neglected all their other frontiers and thrown their whole strength into Natal, they might still have overrun the colony, and exchanged shots at Durban with the fleet itself.

JBA

'THERE IS NO WAY OUT OF THE POLITICAL TROUBLES OF SOUTH AFRICA, EXCEPT REFORM IN THE TRANSVAAL OR WAR.'
MILNER TO CHAMBERLAIN

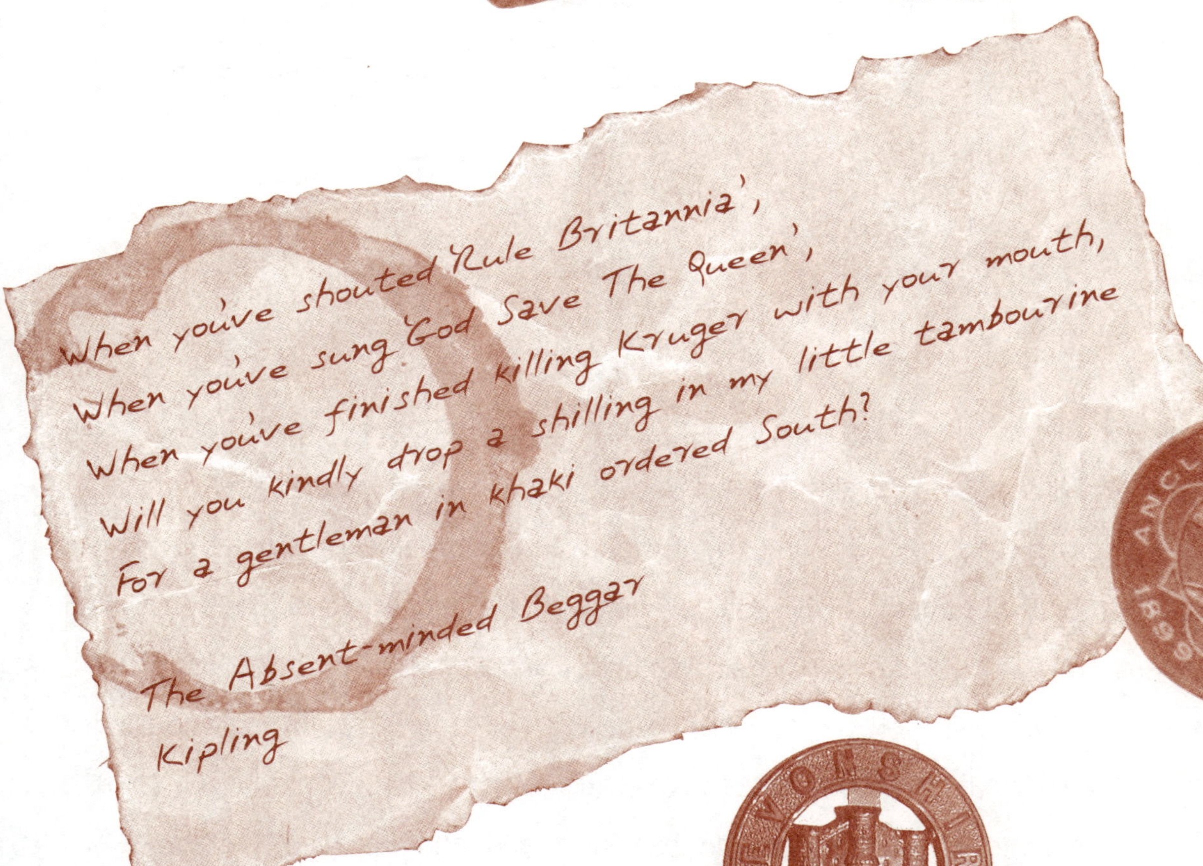

When you've shouted 'Rule Britannia',
When you've sung 'God Save The Queen',
When you've finished killing Kruger with your mouth,
Will you kindly drop a shilling in my little tambourine
For a gentleman in khaki ordered South?

The Absent-minded Beggar
Kipling

In the Transvaal elections of 1898, Kruger was returned to office with more than twice the number of combined votes cast for his two opponents, Joubert and Burger.

'I LOOK ON THIS WAR AS THE SEQUEL OF 1881. I HAVE TOLD THEM ALL THESE YEARS, IT IS NOT FINISHED; WAR MUST COME.' – DOPPER PASTOR

Hymn to Joe

Joe moves in a mysterious way
His trick'ries to perform;
He put our soldiers on the sea,
And yet expects no storm.

Deep in unfathomable craft
And never-failing lies,
He thinks that poor old Kruger's daft,
But lauds Rhodes to the skies.

Judge not our Joe by common sense,
But trust him for his facts,
And for his blundering impudence
Pay extra income tax.

His artful aims are ripening still,
Though all has not been told,
The war may be a bitter pill,
But sweet will be the gold.

PARODY ON 'GOD MOVES IN A MYSTERIOUS WAY' – WILLIAM COWPER – A&M (REVISED) HYMN 181

'A collision with the British is imminent" – DR

1899	**OCTOBER**	**1999**
Sunday *'We hate the English Government' said he to a friend 'and with enough reason, but we do not hate the English people. To the contrary, we hope, that there will come a time in which Dutch and English will work together in unity to the well-being of the whole of South Africa'* – ANDRIES PRETORIUS – VOORTREKKER/BOER LEADER IN KLIPRIVER DISTRICT 1848	**1**	**Friday**
Monday *'The Boer have no feeling about Cape Colony, but they have about Natal; they were driven out of it, and they think it still their own country.'* – DOPPER PASTOR	**2**	**Saturday**
Tuesday *'There were supply dumps at Ladysmith, which caused that place to be selected as the base of the British force composed of troops stationed in Natal and those sent from India.'*	**3**	**Sunday**

'WHEN THE BURGHERS KNEW THAT RHODES WAS NOT PUNISHED THEY LOST ALL TRUST IN ENGLAND.'

General Sir George Stewart White (1835-1912)
Garrison Commander: Ladysmith

George White:

Major (later Field Marshall) 92nd Regiment (later the Gordon Highlanders):

VC Gazetted 2 June 1881

6 October 1879:
Charasiah (Afghan War)

Major White led an attack on a strongly fortified hill where the enemy force outnumbered the major's by about eight to one. When his men became exhausted and immediate action seemed necessary, he took a rifle and, running forward alone, shot the enemy leader. This decided the issue and the enemy fled. Again, at the battle of Kandahar, Major White led the final charge and personally captured one of the two guns held by the enemy, immediately after which the latter retired.

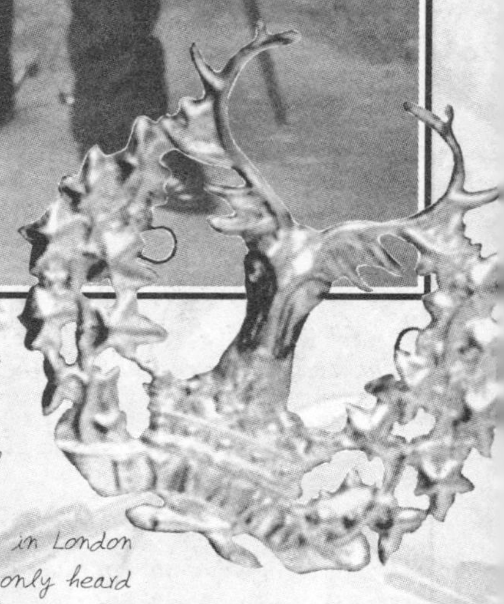

30 October 1899:
Writing to his wife on the eve of their wedding anniversary

'It is doubly sad that the blow of my life has fallen on this day. The newspaper boys are now calling in London the terrible disaster that I have only heard of two hours ago!'

'I must tell you the history of it...'

1899	OCTOBER	1999
Wednesday *'This gold will be your ruin; to remain independent you must remain poor.' – DP*	**4**	Monday
Thursday *'The Transvaal Boer would rather be British Colony than Johannesburg Republic.' – DP*	**5**	Tuesday
Friday *'Little anxiety was felt in England on the outbreak of war.' – JBA*	**6**	Wednesday
Saturday • British army ordered to mobilize • Sir George White lands at Durban	**7**	Thursday
Sunday *'The Boers had let slip their opportunity. Had they sent their ultimatum a month earlier, they might have lost an excuse for war, but they would certainly have conquered a colony!' – JBA*	**8**	Friday
Monday • Boer Ultimatum • General Sir Redvers Buller VC, appointed C-I-C 1st Army Corps	**9**	Saturday
Tuesday • President Kruger's ultimatum, rendering war inevitable, received in London • President Steyn, Orange Free State, throws his lot in with the Z.A.R.	**10**	Sunday

The Victoria cross is unique. It is the supreme award for valour, and no other nation has an exact equivalent to it. It is a decoration without classes or degrees, equally available to all ranks, which is awarded only for individual acts of courage 'in the presence of the enemy'.

JP

First VC of the war

CHARLES FITZCLARENCE: CAPTAIN
(LATER BRIGADIER-GENERAL)
THE ROYAL FUSILIERS
Gazetted 6 July 1900

14 October 1899: Near Mafeking
Captain FitzClarence went with a partially trained squadron to the assistance of an armoured train. The enemy was in greatly superior numbers and the squadron was, for a time, surrounded and in great danger. The Captain, however, so inspired his men that not only was the train relieved, but a heavy defeat was inflicted on the Boers. On 27 October he led his squadron in a successful night attack and on 26 December he again distinguished himself, and was severely wounded.

They paused an instant before they said the word ... 'War', and spoke it softly. It had come at last – the moment they had worked and waited for – and they knew not whether to exult or to despair.

GS

For valour: without courage there is no power on earth to deter an aggressor, nothing to oppose the principle that might is right.

JP

1899	OCTOBER	1999
Wednesday • George White goes to Ladysmith *'None doubted, though many tried to doubt, that at last it was ... WAR!'*	**11**	Monday
Thursday • Boers capture armoured train at Kraaipan • Boers invade Natal via Botha's Pass and cross Western Transvaal border	**12**	Tuesday
Friday *'They hurried hither and thither and arrived nowhither.'*	**13**	Wednesday
Saturday • One VC • Churchill boards HMS *Dunottar Castle* • General Buller embarks at Southampton • Baden-Powell engages Boers outside Mafeking • Boers cut railway near Modder River	**14**	Thursday
Sunday • Martial law proclaimed in Northern Natal	**15**	Friday
Monday • Commandant General Piet Joubert reaches Newcastle • Kimberley and Mafeking invested • Martial law proclaimed in Northern Cape	**16**	Saturday
Tuesday • Parliament assembled • Army Corps mobilized	**17**	Sunday

'True, the Battle of Talana was a British victory, but the British in Dundee were at the mercy of the Boers, who still held Impati and the town water supply and direct escape was inhibited by the Boer capture of Elandslaagte the previous day.'

Elandslaagte: And then in a twinkling, on the stone-pitted, hill-face burst loose that other storm – the storm of lead, of blood, of death. 45

VC

Matthew Meiklejohn:
Captain (later Major)
2nd Batallion The Gordon Highlanders
VC Gazetted 20 July 1900

21 October 1899: Elandslaagte:
After the main Boer position had been captured, some men of the Gordons who were about to assault a kopje were exposed to heavy cross-fire, and having lost their leaders started to waver. Seeing this, Captain Meiklejohn rushed to the front and called on the Gordons to follow him. By this conspicuous bravery and example he rallied the men and led them against the enemy's position, where he fell, desperately wounded in four places.

VC

William Robertson:
Sergeant-Major (later Lieutenant-Colonel)
2nd Batallion The Gordon Highlanders
VC Gazetted 20 July 1900

21 October 1899: Elandslaagte:
During the final advance on the enemy's position, Sergeant-Major Robertson led each successive rush, exposing himself fearlessly to the enemy's artillery and rifle fire to encourage the men. After the main position had been captured, he led a small party to seize the Boer camp. Though exposed to a deadly cross-fire from the enemy's rifles, he gallantly held on to the position captured, and continued to encourage the men until he was dangerously wounded.

Of the I.L.H. Regiment: General Sir Archibald Hunter:
'Every man was a picture of manhood; he was beaming with intelligence.'

VC

Charles Mullins: Captain (later Major) Imperial Light Horse: *Gazetted 12 Feb 1901*
21 October 1899: Elandslaagte: At a most critical moment, when the advance was momentarily checked by very severe fire at point-blank range, Captain Mullins and another officer gallantly rushed forward under very heavy fire and rallied the men, thus enabling the decisive flanking movement to be carried out. Captain Mullins was wounded during the action.

VC

Robert Johnston: Captain (later Major) Imperial Light Horse: *Gazetted 12 Feb 1901*
21 October 1899: Elandslaagte: At a most critical moment, when the advance was momentarily checked by very severe fire at point-blank range, Captain Johnston and another officer gallantly rushed forward under very heavy fire and rallied the men, thus enabling the decisive flanking movement to be carried out.

1899	OCTOBER	1999
Wednesday • Militia reserves called out • Boers occupy Vryburg	18	Monday
Thursday • Boers occupy Elandslaagte and capture supply train • Dismantle railway line	19	Tuesday
Friday • Battle of Talana • French and Haig arrive in Ladysmith	20	Wednesday
Saturday • Four VCs • Battle of Elandslaagte • Mafeking bombarded for four hours – one dog killed	21	Thursday
Sunday • General Yule retires from Dundee to Ladysmith	22	Friday
Monday • Death of General Penn-Symons at Dundee • Boers occupy Dundee	23	Saturday
Tuesday • Battle of Rietfontein • Yule's column approaching Ladysmith 25km to the south	24	Sunday

Times when sound gospel may be poor strategy:

The first big blunder of the Boer War

Monday, 30 October 1899

The Battle of Nicholson's Nek shaped the course of South African history:

'A battle which, for the very fact that it was won by the Republican forces, was more disastrous to the Boer cause than a crushing defeat, and thereby helped to change the destiny of this country. With the lack of vision that marked most of our doings during the first six months of the war, the battle of Modderspruit was hailed by us as a magnificent victory, and, indeed, it certainly was a very striking success, but it would have been better for us in the long run if the British had driven us off that day. In that event we would have adhered to our original plan of campaign and made for Durban instead of sitting down before Ladysmith to a prolonged and useless siege.' DR

VC

John Norwood:
2nd Lieutenant (later Captain)
5th Dragoon Guards: *VC Gazetted 20 July 1900.*

30 October 1899: Ladysmith:

2nd Lieutenant Norwood went out in charge of a small patrol. Having got to within 600 yards of the enemy, they were fired on so heavily that the patrol had to retire at full speed. One man dropped and Norwood galloped back through heavy fire, dismounted and picked up the fallen trooper. He carried him on his back, at the same time leading his horse with one hand. The enemy kept up an incessant fire during the whole of this time.

NOTES:

Mournful Monday was a victory of tactics, a triumph of mobile mounted men over the necessarily slow moving infantry, but by no means a defeat of one army by another. In an action of this nature, one mounted man is calculated to equal three infantrymen.

WSCh

'WHEN GOD HOLDS OUT A FINGER, DON'T TAKE THE WHOLE HAND.'

Our Gallant Foeman:
The Late General Joubert

He was a kindly, well-meaning old man who had done useful service in the smaller campaigns of the past, but he gave me the impression of being bewildered at the heavy responsibility now resting upon him and I felt that he was unequal to the burden.

DR

Joubert's philosophy: Entirely consistent with the Boer attitude to warfare, he was deeply committed to save men's lives, particularly his own, thereby dissatisfying his more impulsive and aggressive followers.

Joubert intended not to assault, but to lay siege to Ladysmith. Encirclement of the town was completed by 3 November, the bulk of the British army in South Africa immobilized in Ladysmith. Major carnage was thus avoided and prospects of British surrender seemed high. Joubert, recalling the military defeat he had inflicted on Britain at Majuba in 1881 and the resulting political concessions, was thus encouraged by the events of Mournful Monday, his own disposition along the lines of the Tugela and concluded that General White was powerless to get out of Ladysmith and General Buller to get through to it.

Joubert was wrong: the British did not surrender and the battle had only just begun.

'TELL ENGLAND, YE WHO PASS THIS MONUMENT, WE WHO DIED SERVING HER, REST HERE CONTENT.'

Corps d'Elite

Leo Amery

The original of the Imperial Light Horse *Tell England* is Simonides (556-468BC) *Select Epigrams*:

> Go, tell the Spartans, thou who passeth by,
> That here obedient to their laws we lie.

The reference is to Marathon.

After the Great War, the then Poet Laureate, Robert Bridges, himself a Worcestershireman, provided further variation at Gheluvelt Chateau (31/10/14) where over 100 Worcesters fell as they charged across open ground into the storm of German fire:

> Asketh thou of these graves?
> They'll tell thee, O Stranger,
> In England,
> How we Worcesters lie where we
> redeemed the battle.

REFERENCE: DR J. FARQUHARSON

Churchill on immunity: 'Inoculation against enteric fever proceeds daily (on board the *Dunottar Castle*). The doctors lecture in the saloon. One injection of the serum protects; a second secures the subject against attacks. Wonderful statistics are quoted in support of the experiment. Nearly everyone is convinced. The operations take place forthwith, and the next day sees haggard forms crawling about the deck in extreme discomfort and high fever. The day after, however, all have recovered and rise gloriously immune. Others, like myself, remembering that we still stand only on the threshold of pathology, remain unconvinced, resolved to trust to "health" and the laws of health! But if they will invent a system of inoculation against bullet wounds I will hasten to submit myself.'

Churchill on the biograph: 'We have a party of cinematographers on board, but the cumbrous appliances take too long to set up ...'

'EVENTS IN THIS PART OF THE FIELD OF WAR HAVE TRIPPED OVER EACH OTHER IN THE RUNNING, AND IT IS DIFFICULT TO MAKE RECORD OF THEM.' – BB

1899	OCTOBER	1999
Wednesday • Telegram received at Simonstown from White asking for naval personnel and guns	**25**	Monday
Thursday • General Yule reaches Ladysmith • Concentration of British forces completed	**26**	Tuesday
Friday • Boers concentrate round Ladysmith	**27**	Wednesday
Saturday • Contingents from Victoria, New South Wales and Tasmania leave for South Africa	**28**	Thursday
Sunday • HMS *Powerful* arrives at Durban • Naval brigade entrains for Ladysmith	**29**	Friday
Monday • One VC • Battle of Ladysmith • Surrender of 850 British at Nicholson's Nek	**30**	Saturday
Tuesday • General Buller lands at Cape Town • Winston Churchill presents himself to Milner then boards the mail train for East London	**31**	Sunday

JANUARY 1862: BULLER, ON SAILING FROM HONG KONG BACK TO BRITAIN, GOT HIS FIRST GLIMPSE OF THE CAPE OF GOOD HOPE.

The Siege of Ladysmith – the Aldershot of South Africa

The siege of Ladysmith has differed from most of the well-known sieges of history in that the garrison, under the officer commanding the forces in Natal, took up a position which he knew to be a weak one, and voluntarily stayed there to be attacked. In most of the great sieges the besieged have had the advantage of holding positions commanding the surrounding country, and the besiegers have had to contend with every difficulty that inferior sites present, and have had, by patient sapping and mining, to push their batteries and trenches up to within effective distance of their opponents' lines. At Ladysmith the position was entirely different. The surrounding hills, which form a wide circle commanding the town, were of necessity relinquished to the Boers. The British held the inner circle, and by constant work and all the skill that their Engineers could bring to bear, made it a position which, if not impregnable, was almost so.

Churchill on Ladysmith: 'The general impression was that Ladysmith was a tremendous strategic position, which dominated the lines of approach both into the Transvaal and the Orange Free State, whereas of course it does nothing of the sort. The fact that it stands at the junction of the railways may have encouraged the belief, but both lines of advance are barred by a broken and tangled country abounding in positions of extraordinary strength. Tactically Ladysmith may be strongly defensible, but for strategic purposes it is absolutely worthless. It is worse. It is a regular trap. The town and cantonment stand in a huge circle of hills which enclasp it on all sides like the arms of a giant, and though so great is the circle that only guns of the heavier class can reach the town from the heights, once an enemy has established himself on these heights it is beyond the power of the garrison to dislodge him, or perhaps even to break out. Not only do the surrounding hills keep the garrison in, but they also form a formidable barrier to the advance of a relieving force. Thus it is that the ten thousand troops in Ladysmith are at this moment actually an encumbrance, and Sir Redvers Buller, who had always deprecated any attempt to hold Natal north of the Tugela, is compelled to attack the enemy on their own terms and their own ground.'

CHAMBERLAIN TO MILNER:

He is a very clever young fellow with many of his father's qualifications.

'WHOEVER SELECTED LADYSMITH AS A MILITARY CENTRE MUST SLEEP UNEASILY AT NIGHTS.' – WSCH

The Aldershot of South Africa:

Ladysmith was selected by a Board of Officers as the site of the great camp in Natal for the same reasons that Aldershot was selected in England. The town stands high, has good water, is healthy, has a plain near it which is an admirable drill ground for all arms, is sheltered to a certain extent by the ring of kopjes and there are several good sites for camps. The officers of the Board who selected the neighbourhood of the town as the site for the camp were not asked to take into account its suitability for a defensive position. Aldershot has never been looked upon as a strong position to hold should England be invaded, and Ladysmith is the Aldershot of Natal.

Extract from *Special Edition Times of Natal*
PIETERMARITZBURG: March 1, 1900

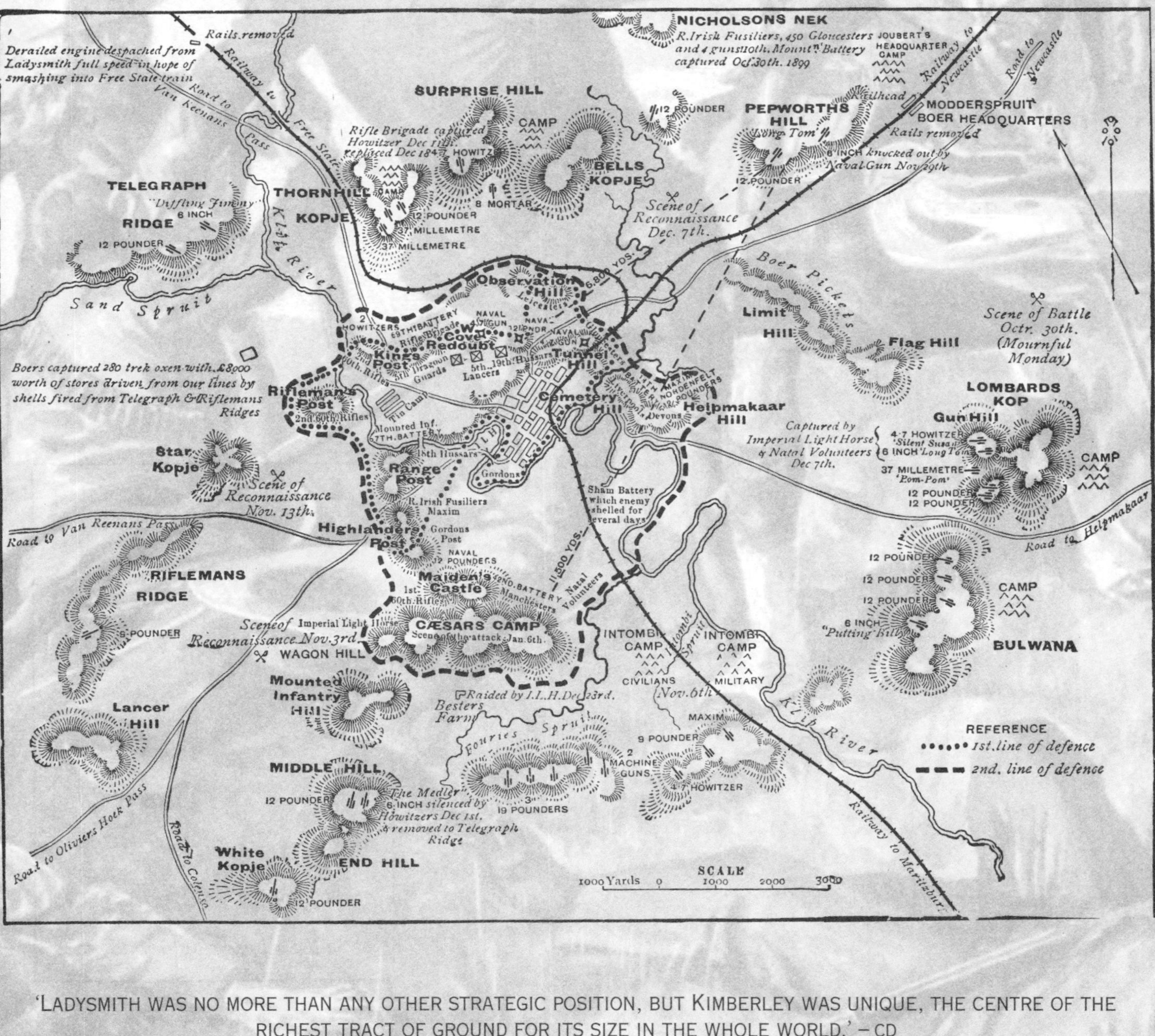

'LADYSMITH WAS NO MORE THAN ANY OTHER STRATEGIC POSITION, BUT KIMBERLEY WAS UNIQUE, THE CENTRE OF THE RICHEST TRACT OF GROUND FOR ITS SIZE IN THE WHOLE WORLD.' – CD

‘HIS GAY, MOCKING SPIRIT AND RIPPLING WIT MADE HIM A DELIGHTFUL COMPANION, AND OUR ACQUAINTANCE RIPENED INTO FRIENDSHIP DURING THE SUMMER MONTHS OF 1899. THIS WAS THE LAST SUMMER HE WAS TO SEE. HE DIED OF TYPHOID FEVER IN LADYSMITH IN THE FOLLOWING JANUARY.’ – WSCH

G W Steevens

‘What Mr Kipling had done for fiction
Mr Steevens did for fact.
He was a priest of the Imperialist idea,
and the glory of the Empire was ever
uppermost in his writings.’

The Unredeemed Curse

Whatever is happening, we are out of it …
We know nothing of the outside: and of the
Inside there is nothing to know.
Weary, stale, flat, unprofitable.
At first to be besieged and bombarded was a thrill,
Then it was a joke; now it is nothing
But a weary, weary, weary, bore.

The siege is an unredeemed curse.

Now we lie in the bottom of the saucer and stare
Up at the pitiless ring of hills that bark death –
Always, always, the same.
You sit here to be idly shot at …
You are of it, but not in it —
Clean out of the world. To your world and to
Yourself you are every bit as good as dead —
Except that dead men have no time to fill in.

45

W. K-L. Dickson says goodbye …

‘IS THE INTEREST DUE TO ANY MERIT IN ME OR IS IT ONLY BECAUSE I AM RANDOLPH’S SON?’ – WSCH

1899	NOVEMBER	1999
Wednesday • Women and children in Ladysmith sent south	**1**	**Monday**
Thursday • Ladysmith invested and bombarded • French and Haig leave on last train out	**2**	**Tuesday**
Friday • HMS *Terrible* leaves Simonstown for Durban • Colenso evacuated by British	**3**	**Wednesday**
Saturday • From East London Churchill wangles a passage on the *Umzimvubu* sailing for Durban • Ladysmith completely cut off • Wessels demands the surrender of Kimberley	**4**	**Thursday**
Sunday • Intombi hospital camp established along railway line outside of Ladysmith	**5**	**Friday**
Monday • Churchill heads by train for Ladysmith • News at Estcourt that Ladysmith is besieged • Sir George White telegraphs 'position entirely safe' (in Ladysmith)	**6**	**Saturday**
Tuesday • Percy Scott appointed Commandant of Durban • Naval Brigade from HMS *Terrible* land	**7**	**Sunday**

The Bombardment

G Steevens

Long Tom – A family of harmless monsters

It was half past seven in the morning of 7 November. The real bombardment, the terrific symphony, had begun.

During the first movement the leading performer was Long Tom. He is a friendly old gun. It was his duty to shell us, and he did; but he did it in an open, manly way.

Behind the half-country of light red soil they had piled up round him you could see his ugly phiz thrust up and look hungrily around. A jet of flame and a spreading toadstool of thick white smoke told us he had fired. On the flash four-point-seven banged his punctilious reply. You waited until you saw the black smoke jump behind the red mound, and then Tom was due in a second or two. A red flash – a jump of red-brown dust and smoke – a rending crash: he had arrived. Then sang slowly through the air his fragments, like wounded birds. You could hear them coming, and they came with dignified slowness: there was plenty of time to get out of the way … It was evident from his conservative use of black powder, and the old-gentlemanly staidness of his movements that he is an elderly gun … Anyhow, he conducted his enforced task with all possible humanity.

On this same 7th a brother Long Tom, by name Fiddling Jimmy, opened on the Manchesters and Caesar's Camp from a flat-topped kopje three of four miles south of them. This gun had been there certainly since the 3rd, when it shelled our returning reconnaissance; but he, too, was a gentle creature, and did little harm to anybody. Next day a third brother, Puffing Billy, made a somewhat bashful first appearance on Bulwan. Four rounds from the four-point-seven silenced him for the day.

In general you may say of the Long Tom family that their favourite habitat is among loose soil on the tops of open hills; they are slow and unwieldy, and very open in all their actions. They are good shooting guns. They are impossible to disable behind their huge epaulements unless you actually hit the gun, and they are so harmless as hardly to be worth disabling.

There were also one or two of their field-guns opposite the Manchesters on the flat-topped hill, one, I fancy, with Long Tom on Pepworth's Hill, and a few others on the northern part of Lombard's Kop and on Surprise Hill to the North-westward.

Westward, on Telegraph Hill, was a gun appeared to prey exclusively on cattle – I am afraid it was one of our own mountain guns turned cannibal. There was a gun on Lombard's Kop called Silent Susan – so called because the shell arrived before the report – a disgusting habit in a gun. The menagerie was completed by the pompoms, of which there were at least three. This noisome beast always lurks in thick bush, whence it barks chains of shell at the unsuspecting stranger. Fortunately its shell is small and it is as timid as it is poisonous.

Altogether, with 3 Long Toms, a 5-inch Howitzer, Silent Susan, – a dozen 12-pounders, four of our screw guns, and three Maxim automatics, they had about two dozen guns on us.

38, 10th Avenue
Northmead
BENONI, Transvaal
15th August 1952

The Town Clerk,
LADYSMITH, Natal.

Dear Sir,

The following is the manner in which the brass telescope (left for you c/o the Royal Hotel) came into my possession.

In the middle of 1901, the 1st Regiment, Kitchener's Fighting Scouts when operating in the Northern Transvaal came into contact with a Boer Commando near Haenertsburg. A few 6 inch shells were fired at the advancing K.F.S. The shells all fell in one straight line showing that something prevented the gun crew from swivelling the gun. It was afterwards ascertained that this was due to the recoil forcing the wheels deep into the soft ground at the side of the road, thus preventing a change in direction of fire. It also prevented its rapid withdrawal in the face of our spread-out advance.

My troop happened to be nearest to the gun site during our charge. On reaching a point about four hundred yards from the emplacement, two violent explosions took place due to charges of dynamite being exploded in both the nozzle and breech of the cannon. The Commando in the meanwhile retreating rapidly from the position, it took less than a minute after the explosion for my troop to reach the damaged gun. I noticed that about thirty 6 inch shells had been placed in a circle with their caps facing a broken case of dynamite to which a lighted coil of fuse was attached. Fortunately, I was in time to withdraw the coil before the dynamite exploded. I then picked up the brass telescope (sent to you) and kept it as a souvenir of the four months I spent in Ladysmith, attached to the A.S.C. during the siege.

During the pursuit of the commando, one of the gun crew was captured. On questioning this man I was told the 6 inch gun and the telescope were the ones used on Umbulwana during the siege of Ladysmith.

At Lord Kitchener's request the damaged 6 inch gun was sent to the Royal Engineers, Pretoria, who re-assembled the broken parts. The same gun was later seen by one of our officers in Hyde Park, London.

Yours faithfully,

AJ Spearman
....
Ex-Lieutenant
1st K.F.S.

12-pounder gun and limber

A Tommy 'Whimsicality'

The Fusiliers that guard this train
Must hold their own with might and main;
Take good aim, and make shots tell,
And send all Dutchmen straight to ...
– a very warm place!

The toughest team sport in the World

THE RUN OUT

(average time 1 min 25 secs)

The guns are raced from the start position down the sides of the arena and manhandled over a five-foot wall. Wooden spars weighing 170lb are erected and wires rigged across the 28-foot chasm. The first men are hauled across, some carrying 120lb wheels over their shoulders. The gun carriage and gun barrels follow, the gun barrels each weighing 900lb. The remainder of the crews, wheels and limbers are pulled over the second wall. Each crew then engages the enemy with three rounds.

THE RUN BACK

(average time 1 min)

All the men and gear have to be withdrawn over the wall and back across the chasm. The combined weight of the gun barrel and gun carriage is 1,250lb; and it goes over in one piece! As soon as the last man of each crew, nicknamed the 'Flying Angel', is across the chasm, the rig is collapsed and three rounds are fired in a rearguard action.

THE RUN HOME

(average time 21 secs)

At the sounding of the 'G' on the bugle the final phase is to take all their equipment through the narrow gaps in the 'Home Wall'. In a matter of seconds the wheels are on, pins are in and the crews go racing flat-out to the finishing line. All three stages are carefully timed and these are added later to the crew's actual running time to give the Official Time for each crew. Each crew now competes seven times against each of the other crews. Only two crews run during each performance. A four-minute run was first recorded in 1948 and a three-minute run in 1962. Nowadays runs in less than three minutes are fairly commonplace, the record being two minutes, 40.6 seconds. The daily results are followed with interest throughout the Royal Navy and are signalled to Ships and Establishments all over the world.

1899	NOVEMBER	1999
Wednesday • 6-inch Creusot gun on Bulwana Hill starts shelling Ladysmith	**8**	Monday
Thursday • Boer attack on Ladysmith repulsed • Garrison fires 21-gun salute: Prince of Wales' birthday	**9**	Tuesday
Friday • Sortie from Estcourt • Boers repulsed	**10**	Wednesday
Saturday • Mobilization of the 5th Division under Sir Charles Warren ordered	**11**	Thursday
Sunday • Armoured train reconnaissance discovers that Boers are approaching Estcourt • Churchill on 'Wilson's death trap' travels to Colenso and back to Estcourt	**12**	Friday
Monday • A party of Boers tearing up the line at Chieveley driven back	**13**	Saturday
Tuesday • Ladysmith Garrison reconnaissance to Rifleman's Ridge	**14**	Sunday

'So they were not cruel men, these enemy.'

Wilson's Death Trap:
'About a mile beyond Frere station towards Colenso lies the wreck of the armoured train – a melancholy heap – one truck on its side (a military cobbler using it as his shop), another upside down with its wheels sticking up in the air, two others standing on the line. There at the curve, at the bottom of the decline down which the train tilted at full speed after the enemy had been seen, is the broken rail successfully designed to send the train to destruction; and there on either side of the line are the ridges, profitably close, from which the Boers poured their fire. The trucks are ripped through and through with shells – the holes round and clean as a whistle where the shells came in, and jagged and gaping where they passed out – and spattered over with the marks of lead. And beside the wreckage is a more melancholy sight still – the little mound that covers impartially the poor fellows of the Dublin Fusiliers and the Durban Light Infantry who were killed and buried by the enemy.'

Round the grave the devotion of the Border Regiment has placed a stone border, and at the head erected a tombstone and a little cross of wire. On the tombstone are chiselled the words:

HERE LIETH THE REMAINS OF THOSE WHO WERE KILLED IN THE ARMOURED TRAIN ON NOV. 15TH, 1899

On the grave itself there is studded with empty cartridge cases, many of course used by the dead men themselves, this inscription:

ERECTED BY THE BORDER REGIMENT IN MEMORY OF OUR COMRADES

Here, one foresees, is a monument destined to last, destined to be renewed when it becomes obscure, and always to provide a Mecca for the excursionist.
JBA

The grave has been carefully tended over the years and remains a Mecca for all those who visit the site.

Captain Aylmer Haldane

One of the many acquaintances that Churchill had met at Estcourt was a friend from his North West Frontier days: the tall, heavily moustached Captain Haldane who had been wounded at Elandslaagte. Temporarily attached to the Royal Dublin Fusiliers until he could rejoin his battalion of the Gordon Highlanders in Ladysmith, Haldane informed Churchill that he had been ordered to take out the armoured train the following morning to support the cavalry reconnaissances. As Churchill had already been out in the train and knew the country as far as Colenso, Haldane invited him to join the expedition. Both, initially condemning the assignment as 'the height of folly', yet, having a feeling, an intuition 'that something will come of it', arranged to meet early the following morning.

'THE FIRST – AND LAST – TIME IN HIS LIFE THAT CHURCHILL SURRENDERED.'
'THE LAST SEEN OF HIM WAS AS HE TRUDGED ALONE AWAY DOWN INTO THE ARENA OF BATTLE, WHERE THE SHOT AND SHELL WERE STILL SCREAMING, SPLINTERING ROCK AND PLOUGHING THE GROUND.' – BB

1899	NOVEMBER	1999
Wednesday • Armoured train wrecked by Boers near Frere • Winston Churchill captured by Veld-Cornet Sarel Oosthuizen and marched to Colenso	**15**	Monday
Thursday • Hildyard arrives at Estcourt with re-inforcements • Bridge over the Tugela destroyed by the Boers • P.O.W. marched to Boer HQ outside Ladysmith	**16**	Tuesday
Friday • Boers occupy Weenen • Botha reported to be 5 miles north-west of Estcourt • P.O.W. marched to Modderspruit Railway Station	**17**	Wednesday
Saturday • Boers attack Estcourt *KRUGER: 'They might as well let him go as one man could do no harm.'* *– Too late, as P.O.W. on train to Pretoria.*	**18**	Thursday
Sunday • Churchill and Haldane locked up in the Staatsmodel school in Pretoria *'Whirr—whizz—e-e-e-e—phutt!!'*	**19**	Friday
Monday • General French arrives at Naauwpoort • Denys Reitz accompanies his father, Transvaal State Attorney, when he visits Churchill	**20**	Saturday
Tuesday • Estcourt under General Hildyard isolated, the Boers having occupied Highlands Station on the railway to the south • Mooi River camp shelled	**21**	Sunday

'WHEN ONE IS ALONE AND UNARMED, A SURRENDER MAY BE PARDONED.' – NAPOLEON

Facsimile of a newspaper published in Ladysmith during the siege.

THE LADYSMITH LYRE.

"Let him Lie." – *Old Song.*

Vol. I. No. 1. 27th NOVEMBER, 1899. PRICE – 6D

PROSPECTUS:

The *Ladysmith Lyre* is published to supply a long felt want. What you want in a besieged town, cut off from the world, is news which you can absolutely rely on as false. The rumours that pass from tongue to tongue may, for all you know, be occasionally true. Our news we guarantee to be false.

In the collection and preparation of falsehoods we shall spare no effort and no expense. It is enough for us that Ladysmith wants stories; it shall have them.

It is possible, however, even in the best regulated newspaper that some truths may unavoidably creep in. To save our readers the trouble of picking them out, these will be published in a special column by themselves. This division of news, into true and false, is an entirely new departure in the history of the public press. Whatever you read in the space devoted to truth, you may believe. The rest of the *Ladysmith Lyre* you my believe, or not, as you like.

LATEST LYRES.

FROM OUR OWN DESPONDENTS.

(BY WIRELESS TELEGRAPHY).

London, November 5.

A shell from Long Tom burst in the War Office this afternoon. General Brackenbury, Directory General of Ornance, accepted its arrival with resignation. Several reputations were seriously damaged. Unfortunately the Ornance Committee was not sitting. A splinter broke into the foreign office and disturbed the siesta of the Prime Minister.

Mr. A.J. Balfour has prepared a third edition of "Philosophic Doubt." The work contains a new chapter on the doubts entertained by the Cabinet as to the probabilities of war with the Transvaal. The First Lord of the Treasury has dedicated the edition to his uncle, Lord Salisbury.

The artillery intended for the campaign in South Africa will be despatched as soon as the necessary ammunition has been received from the German factories.

The Lord Mayor has appointed a Mansion House Committee for the relief of Ladysmith.

Mr. Michael Davitt, Dr. Tanner, Mr. Dillon and Mr. Swift McNeill have announced their intention of joining the Irish Brigade. The House of Commons, without demur, voted a grant in aid.

The Second Army Corps has been discovered in the pigeon holes of the War Office.

Omdurman, November 13.

The Khalifa has returned to his palace on the Nile. Lord Kitchener is at Fashoda. He is marching south to raise the siege of Ladysmith.

Paris, November 10.

Major Marchand has organised an expedition to the sources of the Klip River. It is rumoured that his object is to prevent the junction of the British forces north and south of the Tugela. The Government of the Republic has been warned that this will be regarded as "an unfriendly act."

The exhibition has been put off until the end of the 20th century in order that France may devote her energies to the subjugation of great Britain.

Adis Adba, November 2.

Menelik has declared war against France. He has appealed to Great Britain for assistance.

Later.

I am informed on the highest authority that Menelik has declared war against Great Britain, and has appealed to France for assistance.

Johannesburg, November 19.

Having learned through the medium of *The Standard Diggers' News* that the Johannesburg commando are settled in Ladysmtih with either wives and families, several hundred vrouwen left hurriedly for Natal this morning. New and interesting developments are anticipated.

St.Petersburg, November 20.

The Czar has issued invitations to another Peace Conference Pretoria is mentioned as the probable meeting place. President Kruger has intimated that the south African Republic will not be represented.

Vienna, April 1.

News has reached here from a reliable source that Lord Salisbury has agreed to the terms of peace proposed, by President Kruger – the surrender of that part of Natal now occupied by the Boers.

—— o ——

LOCAL INTELLIGENCE.

General Clery has withdrawn his relieving column to the Mooi River. Marizburg is almost deserted. Joubert has gone south with the greater part of his force.

General Buller is at Cape Town. General French is not at Dundee. Through cable rates from Ladysmith to London have been reduced to 3d. per word. The Town Guard are undermining Umbulwani. They propose to blow up the enemy's guns with cyanide of potassium. The Resident magistrate at Intombi Camp has sent for his horses. He is deeply touched by the reception given to his sackful of letters and despatches. Mr. Schalk Burger has sent a protest against the Red Cross flag on the hospital at the Town Hall. He has since emphasised the protest by shelling the flat. General Joubert has been invited to dismantle the forts on Pepworth and Umbulwani, and to send in as prisoners the gunners who hoisted the white flag over Long Tom and his brother Puffing Billy, in order that they may load and lay the guns in safety. Mrs. Kruger, whose health is excellent, complains that the President is becoming too English. He no longer goes to bed in hat and boots.

—— o ——

CHRISTMAS PUDDINGS!

CHRISTMAS PUDDINGS!!

OUR PRIZE COMPETITION.

Do you want a Christmas pudding? You will! This is how you can get it.

This prize will be given for

THE MOST MIRACULOUS ESCAPE

from the shell fire of the enemy between the dates of November 2 and December 20. The competition will close on December 21st at 12 noon.

So if you want a Christmas pudding delay no longer. Go out and have a miraculous escape and send a description of it to

The editor of the *Ladysmtih Lyre*,
c/o the Manager of the *Ladysmith Lyre*,
c/o Mrs. Haydon,
Main Street,
Near 21st Street, F.B.,
Ladysmith

'IS IT NOT A LITTLE ODD THAT THE WAR OFFICE HAS FORGOTTEN TO PROVIDE THE OFFICERS WITH A SUPPLY OF MILITARY MAPS OF NATAL?' – BB

1899	NOVEMBER	1999
Wednesday • Buller leaves Cape Town for Natal • Boers shell Mooi River	**22**	Monday
Thursday • Action at Willow Grange • Boers driven from their position on Beacon Hill • Churchill complains to a Reuter's correspondent	**23**	Tuesday
Friday • Boer retreat from Willow Grange • Piet Joubert badly injured by fall	**24**	Wednesday
Saturday • General Buller arrives at Maritzburg • The Boers fall back on the Tugela • Churchill visited by the American Consul in Pretoria	**25**	Thursday
Sunday • First issue of *The Ladysmith Lyre* news-sheet published	**26**	Friday
Monday • Naval Brigade from HMS *Terrible* leaves Durban to join Buller's force at Frere	**27**	Saturday
Tuesday • Battle of Modder River • Lord Methuen's third assault on Boer position	**28**	Sunday

'OH, ALMIGHTY GOD, WHY HAST THOU GIVEN ME A FOOL FOR MY FIRST-BORN?' – COL. HAMILTON
(THE VERY SENTIMENTS OF RANDOLPH CHURCHILL)

Ian Standish Monteith Hamilton: 1853-1947

Born at Corfu, he was the eldest son of Colonel Christian Monteith Hamilton, C.O. 92nd Gordon Highlanders. Educated at Cheam and Wellington College, he entered the army in 1873, serving with the 92nd Gordon Highlanders in the Afghan War 1873-80, and was present at the operations around Cabul, December 1979. As a captain he joined the staff of Sir Frederick Roberts, then Commander-in-Chief at Madras, as ADC; served in the Boer War 1881; with the Nile Expedition 1886-7, with Sir Frederick Roberts Staff; Colonel 1891; Military Secretary to General Sir George White; with the Chitral Relief Force 1895; Commanded the 3rd Brigade, Tirah Expeditionary Force, 1897-8; Commandant of the School of Musketry, Hythe 1898; and held this post till he embarked for South Africa with Sir George White.

Nobody, not even Lord Bobs in all his glory, has touched my life at so many points as Winston Churchill.

Winston Leonard Spencer Churchill: 1874-1965

The eldest son of the late Lord Randolph Churchill, he inherited many of his father's brilliant qualities. Educated at Harrow and Sandhurst, he entered the army 1895, serving with the Spanish Forces in Cuba that year, and saw much Indian service with the Malakand Field Force in 1897; was Orderly Officer to the Late Sir William Lockhart, and was attached to the 21st Lancers with the Nile Expeditionary Force in 1898, and present at the Battle of Khartoum. Churchill, having dared to criticize Kitchener in his second book, *The River War*, all journalists were banned from having rank. Winston therefore had to resign his commission as Second Lieutenant in the 4th Hussars in order to come to South Africa as Correspondent for *The Morning Post*.

'Brother! Equal! Ugh! Free! Not a bit!'

Here, Churchill felt, was the fundamental cause of the Boers' dislike of British rule. Not past conflicts, not Majuba or the Jameson Raid, but the difference in attitude towards the African was at the root of the enmity between the two white races.

'BRITISH GOVERNMENT IS ASSOCIATED IN THE BOER FARMER'S MIND, WITH VIOLENT SOCIAL REVOLUTION. BLACK IS TO BE PROCLAIMED THE SAME AS WHITE. THE SERVANT IS TO BE RAISED AGAINST THE MASTER; THE AFRICAN TO BE CONSTITUTED HIS LEGAL EQUAL, TO BE ARMED WITH POLITICAL RIGHTS.' – WSCH

1899	NOVEMBER	1999
Wednesday • First Canadian Contingent arrives at Cape Town	**29**	**Monday**
Thursday • Heavy bombardment of Ladysmith • Sixth Division announced for South Africa • Churchill turns 25	**30**	**Tuesday**

30 Nov 1874 - Winston Leonard Spencer Churchill:

Yet nothing in his childhood or his youth
Pointed to Winston Churchill's diverse talents
Or to the destiny which awaited him.
His life would span two eras:
As a young man he would ride in the Last Cavalry Charge of History;
After entering politics, and years of fluctuating fortunes,
His finest hour would also be Britain's.
Hailed as his country's saviour,
He was to live on to a vigorous old age,
And attend upon the dawning of the Nuclear Age.

Mary Soames
(Youngest daughter)

Buller's Lament ...

Here I am, condemned to fight in Natal,
Which all my judgment has told me to avoid,
And try to advance along the line worst
Of all suited to our troops..

Age, easy living, heaviness of body, many years of promotion and success in times of peace, dissipate the vital forces indispensable to intense action.

He is a stern, fighting soldier, as well as an experienced and masterly leader of troops, who will stand no nonsense nor brook incapables. With him in the field the Boers' long innings will be finally closed

BB

Redvers Henry Buller:

The son of a Devonshire squire, MP for a division of the county, owner of the manor of Downes, near Crediton, Devonshire, was born 7 Dec 1839. He attended Eton after 'disgracing himself at Harrow'. He lost his mother when he was only 16. She died in his arms of 'haemorrhage of the lungs'.

Buller should have had every reason for confidence; after all, he was going to South Africa at the head of the largest, and best equipped, military expedition that had ever left England.

Redvers Buller: VC; GCB; GCMG:
Family connection with 2nd Lieutenant A. B. Turner, VC and Lieutenant-Colonel B. V. Turner, VC; in command Aldershot 1898-99; served in South Africa 1899-1900 as General Commanding Forces and then as GOC in Natal; commanded 1st Army Corps, Aldershot 1901.

'Hours crawl like paralytic centipedes.' – WSCH

'IN NATAL A YOUNG STRATEGIST WAS EMERGING IN THE HANDSOME PERSON OF LOUIS BOTHA, DOTED UPON BY GENERALS LUKAS MEYER AND PIET JOUBERT.' – JM

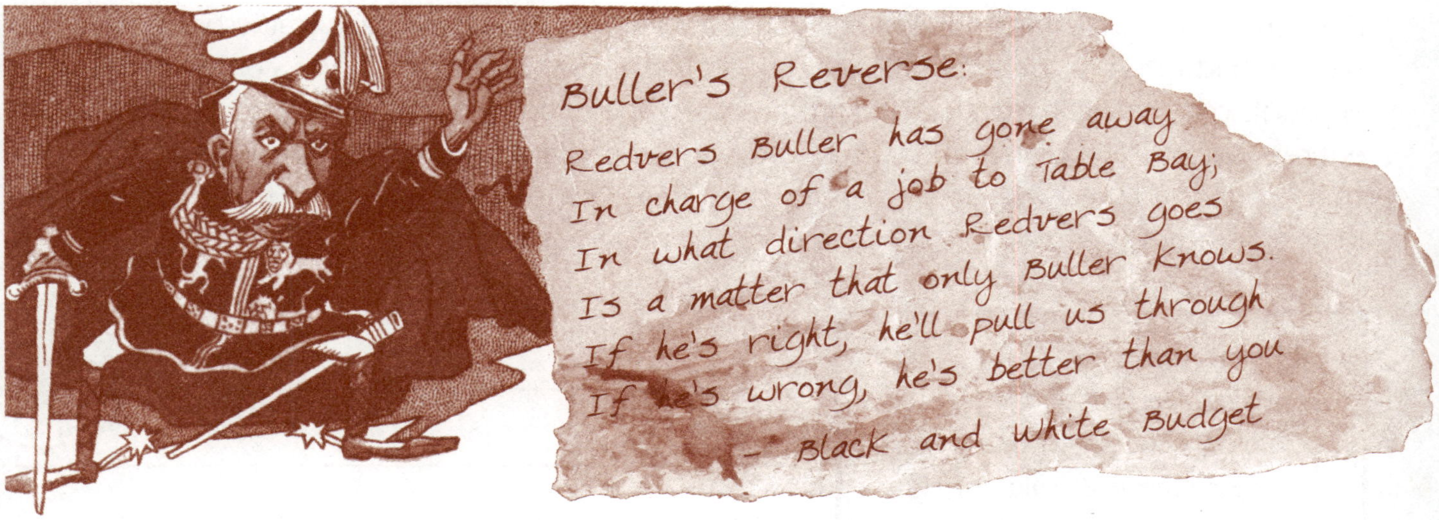

1899	DECEMBER	1999
Friday • Long Tom starts firing from Gun Hill • Haldane and Brockie reach definite decision to break out on their own	1	Wednesday
Saturday *'Also their guns, being newer, better pieces, mounted on higher ground, outranged ours.'*	2	Thursday
Sunday *'We had more guns, but they were as useless as catapults: only the six naval guns could touch Pepworth's Hill or Bulwan.'*	3	Friday
Monday • Boers advance and entrench at Magersfontein • Haldane and Brockie begin to accumulate food and plan route out of Transvaal	4	Saturday
Tuesday • Buller arrives at Frere base camp	5	Sunday

BULLER VC: 60TH K.R.R. 'KEENEST AND GREATEST OF RIFLEMEN.'

Boers reasoned that Winston Churchill had forfeited his non-combatant status because of the part he had taken in the armoured train fight. Natal newspapers, however, contained glowing accounts of Churchill's activities, and attributed escape of both the locomotive and the wounded entirely to him. General Joubert therefore intimated that although Churchill had not fired a shot, he had injured the Boer operations by freeing the locomotive and must therefore be treated as a prisoner-of-war. This made Churchill resolve to escape.

Ineffectiveness of bombardment:

i) Timing was usually predictable: breaks for meals; seldom any firing after dark; and, in accordance with Boer religious principles, never onSundays.

ii) Bombardment not properly co-ordinated.

iii) Guns were outside shrapnel range and common shells were mostly either blind or smothered in soft ground.

NOTES:

VC

Henry Douglas:

Lieutenant (later Major-General) Royal Army Medical Corps:
Gazetted 29 March 1901

11 Dec 1899: Magersfontein: Lieutenant Douglas went out in the open and attended to wounded officers and men under intense enemy fire. He performed many similar acts of gallantry on the same day.

VC

John Shaul:

Corporal (later Bugle-Major): 1st Batallion The Highland Light Infantry:
Gazetted 28 Sep 1900

11 December 1899: Magersfontein: Corporal Shaul was in charge of stretcher-bearers, but at one period of the battle he was seen encouraging men to advance across the open. He was most conspicuous during the day in dressing men's wounds and in one case he came, under fire, to a man who was lying wounded in the back, and with the utmost coolness sat down beside him and proceeded to dress his wound. This act of gallantry was performed under continuous fire as calmly as if there had been no enemy near.

1899	DECEMBER	1999
Wednesday • General Schalk Burger succeeds Piet Joubert in command of Boers at Ladysmith	**6**	Monday
Thursday • Haldane and Brockie experience a set-back. Two soldier servants, Cahill and Bridges, usurp their plan and escape unnoticed • Sortie under General Hunter destroys two Boer guns on Gun Hill	**7**	Tuesday
Friday • Haldane does not want Churchill in on escape • Sortie returns to Ladysmith with Long Tom breech block and a Maxim gun	**8**	Wednesday
Saturday • Haldane under obligation, but Churchill, the most conspicuous prisoner in the Staatsmodel school, would attract attention *'Few shells fell in town, and of the few many were half-charged with coal-dust, and many never burst at all.'*	**9**	Thursday
Sunday • Churchill included in planning escape • Reverse at Stormberg; start of Black Week • Successful sortie from Ladysmith and capture of Surprise Hill	**10**	Friday
Monday • Two VCs • Battle of Magersfontein – General Wauchope killed • Digby-Jones RE destroys Boer howitzer on Surprise Hill • 7 o'clock: Plans for first attempt to escape abandoned	**11**	Saturday
Tuesday • The Union Brigade – English, Scottish, Irish and Welsh Fusiliers begin the advance on Colenso from Frere • Second attempt planned: Haldane postpones • Churchill escapes alone and boards a train	**12**	Sunday

VC

Walter Congreve: Captain (later Lieutenant-General): The Rifle Brigade: *Gazetted 2 Feb 1900*

15 December 1899: Colenso: Captain Congreve, with several others, tried to save the guns of the 14th and 66th Batteries, RFA, when the detachments serving the guns had all become casualties or been driven from their guns. Some of the horses and drivers were sheltering in a donga about 500 yards behind the guns and the intervening space was swept with shell and rifle fire. Captain Congreve, with two other officers, (Schofield and Babtie) helped to hook a team into a limber and then to limber up a gun. Although wounded himself, seeing one of the officers fall, (Fred Roberts), he went out with an RAMC Major (Babtie) and brought him in.

VC

William Babtie: Major (Later Lieutenant-General: Royal Army Medical Corps: *Gazetted 20 April 1900*

15 December 1899: Colenso: Major Babtie rode up under heavy rifle fire to attend to the wounded who were lying in an advanced donga close to the rear of the guns. When he arrived at the donga, he attended to them all, going from place to place, exposed to the heavy rifle fire which greeted anyone who showed himself. Later in the day Major Babtie went out with another officer (Congreve) to bring in Lieutenant The Honourable Freddie Roberts, who was lying on the veld – this also under very heavy fire.

VC

Harry Schofield: Captain (later Lieutenant-Colonel) RFA: *Gazetted 30 August 1901*

15 December 1899: Colenso: Captain Schofield, with several others, tried to save the guns of the 14th and 66th Batteries, RFA, when the detachments serving the guns had all become casualties or been driven from their guns by infantry fire at close range. Captain Schofield went out with two other officers and a corporal (Congreve, Roberts and Nurse respectively) when the first attempt was made to extricate the guns; and helped in withdrawing the two that were saved.

VC

Frederick Hugh Roberts: The Honourable Lieutenant: The King's Royal Rifle Corps: *Gazetted 2 Feb 1900*

15 December 1899: Colenso: Lieutenant Roberts, with several others, tried to save the guns of the 14th and 66th Batteries, RFA, when the detachments serving the guns had all become casualties or been driven from their guns. Some of the horses and drivers were sheltering in a donga about 500 yards behind the guns and the intervening space was swept with shell and rifle fire. Lieutenant Roberts with two other officers, Congreve and Schofield, helped to hook a team into a limber and then to limber up a gun. While doing so; he fell badly wounded and later died of his wounds.

VC

Hamilton Reed: Captain (later Major-General): 7th Battery RFA: *Gazetted 2 February 1900*

15 December 1899: Colenso: When so many horses had become casualties, Captain Reed brought three teams from his battery in an attempt to save the remaining guns. The shell and rifle fire was intense and he was wounded almost at once, as were five of the 13 men who rode with him. One was killed and 13 horses out of 21 (including his own), were killed before he got half way to the guns, and he was forced to retire.

VC

George Nurse: Corporal (later 2nd Lieutenant): 66th Battery, RFA: *Gazetted 2 February 1900*

15 December 1909: Colenso: Corporal Nurse, with several others, tried to save the guns of the 14th and 66th Batteries, RFA, when the detachments serving the guns had all become casualties or been driven from their guns. Some of the horses and drivers were sheltering in a donga about 500 yards behind the guns and the intervening space was swept with shell fire. Corporal Nurse, with three officers (Congreve, Roberts and Schofield), helped to hook a team into a limber, and then to limber up a gun. Then, on is own, he managed to limber up a second gun.

VC

George Ravenhill: Private: 2nd Batallion, The Royal Scots Fusiliers: *Gazetted 4 June 1901*

15 December 1899: Colenso: Private Ravenhill went several times under heavy fire from his sheltered position as one of the escort to the guns to assist the officers and drivers who were trying to withdraw a number of guns when the detachments serving them had all been killed, wounded or driven from them by infantry fire at close range. Private Ravenhill also helped to limber up one of the guns which was saved.

1899	DECEMBER	1999
Wednesday • The railway ran towards the rising sun. After dark Churchill walked towards a coal mine • British guns open on the Boer position at Colenso • Charles Warren at Cape Town	**13**	Monday
Thursday • Buller decides on a frontal attack on Colenso • At dawn Churchill is taken down a shaft and left in a small recess	**14**	Tuesday
Friday • Seven VC's • Disaster at Colenso: the biggest loss recorded to date in South African war *'The underground hideout was infested with rats: white rats with pink eyes.'*	**15**	Wednesday
Saturday • Black Week culminates in Buller being demoted to C-I-C Natal Force only *'The three days I passed in the mine were not among the most pleasant which my memory re-illuminates.'*	**16**	Thursday
Sunday • Churchill is taken on a tour of the mine • Lord Roberts appointed C-I-C in South Africa with Lord Kitchener as his Chief of Staff • Large reinforcements ordered out	**17**	Friday
Monday • The escape plan is devised • General Piet Joubert reported to have resumed command of Boer forces in Natal	**18**	Saturday
Tuesday • Just after two in the morning Churchill crawled into hiding on a goods truck *'Our naval friends succeed in smashing the Colenso bridge.'*	**19**	Sunday

Churchill: He saw much in Boerland, and did something, and got caught; but being quick-witted, lithe, active, and perhaps lucky, he was able to escape from Pretoria in a manner which caused some sensation and made him the hero of an hour. He is a clever fellow who has the courage of his opinions; yet he thinks that the Boer is not so black as he is painted.

A Gentleman's War!

'What garrison have you at Estcourt?' a Boer officer asked Churchill.

'Forgive me,' was the answer, given in the tone of all the conversation, 'but is that, do you think a fair question to ask me, even though I am a prisoner?'

'I beg your pardon,' said the Boer; 'I should not have asked it.'

And it was not asked again.

JBA

VC

Horace Martineau: Sergeant (later Lieutenant) Protectorate Regiment (NW CC), SA Forces: *Gazetted 6 July 1900*

26 December 1899: Near Mafeking: During the action at Game Tree, when the order to retire had been given, Sergeant Martineau rescued a corporal who had been struck down near the Boer trenches. The sergeant managed to half-drag, half-carry the wounded man to a bush where he attended to his wounds. He was shot in the side himself but took no notice and carried on helping the corporal until he was wounded a second time and was forced to give up.

VC awarded for saving his brother's life

VC

Horace Ramsden: Trooper: Protectorate (NW CC) SA Forces: *Gazetted 6 July 1900*

26 December 1899: Near Mafeking: During the action at Game Tree, after the order to retire had been given, Trooper Ramsden picked up his brother who had been shot through both legs and was lying some 10 yds from the Boer trenches. He carried him about 600 to 800 yds under heavy fire (putting him down from time to time to rest) until help arrived and the injured man was carried to a place of safety.

'OUR CHRISTMAS DINNER WAS ONE TO BE REMEMBERED: THERE WAS TOO LITTLE TO FORGET.' – N.M.R.

1899	DECEMBER	1999
Wednesday • Anxious waiting: helplessness • Formation of City of London Imperial Volunteers for South Africa announced	**20**	Monday
Thursday • Charles Warren leaves Cape Town for Natal • White's Ladysmith HQ bombed out *'As we rumbled and banged along, I pushed my head out of the tarpaulin and sang and shouted and crowed at the top of my voice.'*	**21**	Tuesday
Friday • The SS *Induna* departs from Lorenzo Marques early morning with Churchill aboard *'As fast as they build (entrenchments) we endeavour to destroy.'*	**22**	Wednesday
Saturday • Lord Roberts departs for South Africa • Winston Churchill lands at Durban after escaping from Boer captivity *'He was definitely, and permanently Winston!'*	**23**	Thursday
Sunday *'The greatest indignity of my life!: Mr Churchill had returned to us, his quarters being the platelayer's hut which stood within a hundred yards of the spot where he had been captured some six weeks earlier.'*	**24**	Friday
Monday • Christmas day tacitly observed as a truce at Ladysmith *'Winston Churchill was established forthwith as one of those people about whom everybody talked, joked, or disputed, and at the mention of whose name people got violently excited.'*	**25**	Saturday
Tuesday • Two VC's • Lord Methuen's third assault on Boer position BOXING DAY: *'A great many of us are suffering from the effects of the Christmas dinner. Not too much, but the sudden change from a plain diet to a rich one.'*	**26**	Sunday

'IMAGINE HIM QUALIFYING FOR THE BAR OR CUTTING A FIGURE IN POLITICS ... THE ARMY IS ALL THAT'S LEFT.' – RCH.

Siegetown Christmas Party

*Major Karri-Davies gave an account of how the **Ladysmith Siege Christmas Tree** came about:*

Colonel Dartnell and I were discussing how we could give the little ones of Ladysmith, most of whom had been living for the past two months in holes by the river bank, as happy a time as might be possible under the novel circumstances. Owing to the shelling which the town was subject to, it was quite out of the question to gather the young people together during the day time, so we decided that the best thing to do was to have a Christmas Tree Party.

We accordingly searched the town and persuaded the proprietors of some of the shops to open up and sell us all sorts of suitable goods to hang on the tree. Then we called in Mr George Tatham who very kindly agreed to lend us his hall, while his wife volunteered to assist in the decoration of the Tree and to look after the supper if we could procure the ingredients and materials for the feast. Archdeacon Barker whom we next visited to ensure that our arrangements for a party on Christmas night did not interfere with his arrangements, also volunteered his help, with that of his wife and daughter.

While looking for a suitable tree, I found the orthodox English Christmas tree growing side by side with the bluegum of Australia and the mimosa of South Africa. It immediately struck me that Mother Earth's suggestion was the right one and that since the soldiers of all parts of the Empire were fighting side by side, it would be appropriate to have the Empire botanically represented by Christmas trees grown on South African soil. With the assistance of the officers and men of the Natal Mounted Police and the Imperial Light Horse, we placed the trees in position in the hall.

Major Doveton arrived and immediately said: 'Where's Canada? She must be represented.' Off he went to return later with a huge Canadian fir tree. Colonel Dartnell and Miss Olive Barker - the daughter of the Anglican Archdeacon Barker - took charge of the South African tree and the rest of us dressed the other trees. We felt that with the valuable assistance of 120 pounds of sweets, together with mountains of cakes, lemonade and ginger beer, we were ready to welcome as many young guests as Ladysmith could provide. Of course, there were many sick children, but they were not forgotten and presents were put aside for them.

At half past seven the door of the hall was opened. As they entered each child was given a ticket to present at the Tree for gifts. In less than an hour all of the children - about 250 - had received three or four presents each. The General and his Staff were good enough to come and join in the fun. After refreshments had been served the hall was cleared and dancing was kept up until eleven o'clock, when we all joined in singing 'God save the Queen'.

'A DECISION ONCE TAKEN SHOULD NOT BE GIVEN UP.' – GANDHI

1899	**DECEMBER** **1999**
Wednesday *'Our sailor lads and Tommies got a good bath by stripping and running about in the rain.'*	**27** Monday
Thursday • HMS *Magicienne* captured the German liner *Bundesrath* near Delagoa Bay	**28** Tuesday
Friday • Daily bombardment of Ladysmith growing heavier: shell fire continuous	**29** Wednesday
Saturday *'White was fortunate in the troops he commanded – half of them old soldiers from India.' – CD*	**30** Thursday
Sunday *'We are again without food for our horses, and there is none to be had for love or money.'*	**31** Friday

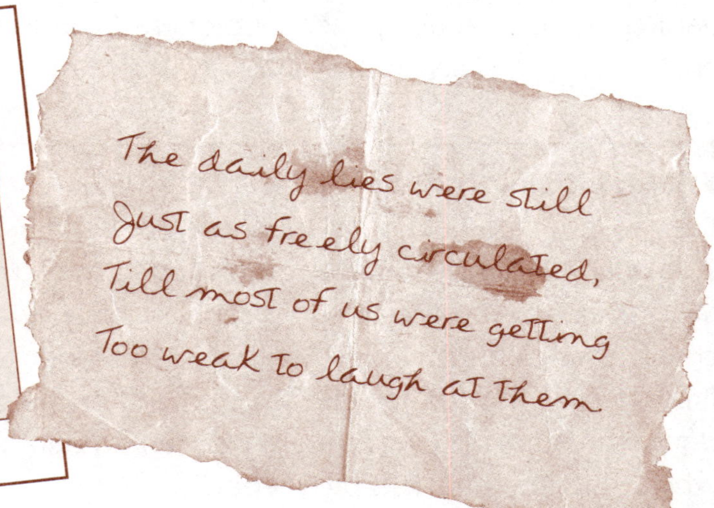

The Jameson Raid

The Raid made Steyn's election as President a certainty. Fraser was a good man and none could doubt his loyalty to the Free State or the fact that he had served the country well, but, and it was a very big but, he was English, and the English had again betrayed their pledges. The Jameson Raid might well be the beginning of a more serious attempt to gain the Gold Fields, and if it happened, the Free State wanted a man who would have no divided loyalties as President.

Dr Leander Starr Jameson CB: 'He is Scotch but not aggressively Scotch. He was born at Edinburgh, and he is 43 years old and a Medical doctor. Like Mr Cecil Rhodes he went to South Africa for his health's sake, and practised to such purpose in Kimberley that he was presently making some five or six thousand a year. For years he lived under the same roof with Mr Rhodes. Being fully trusted by Mr Rhodes he long since was the bearer of his Power of Attorney which gave him a very high position all over South Africa. But President Kruger does not like him. He has been called a raider, a free-booter, a filibuster and other hard names. He has suffered much with alacrity for what he holds to be a right cause. Recent events have made him the most popular man in the Empire. He has a charm of manner so magnetic in its effect that he is said to be able to subdue the wildest of savages.'

Frederick Sleigh Roberts

VC, KG, KP, GCB, OM, GCSI, GCIE, VD

Father of Lieutenant The Honourable F.H.S. Roberts, VC; QM General in India 1875-78; C-I-C Madras 1881-85; C-I-C India 1885-93; Commander, Forces in Ireland 1895; C-I-C SA 1899-1900; C-I-C 1901-04; Colonel in Chief Overseas and Indian Forces in Europe 1914; Colonel-Commandant, Royal Regiment of Artillery 1896; Colonel of the Irish Guards 1900; Knight of the order of St John.

VC

Frederick Sleigh Roberts:

Lieutenant (later Field Marshall and Earl): Bengal Artillery: *Gazetted 24 Dec 1858*

2 January 1858: Khodagunge (India): On following up the retreating enemy, Lieutenant Roberts saw in the distance two sepoys going away with a standard. He immediately gave chase, overtaking them just as they were about to enter a village. Although one of them fired at him, the Lieutenant was not hit and he took possession of the standard, cutting down the man who was carrying it. He had also on the same day saved the life of a sowar who was being attacked by a sepoy.

'AS A FIELD COMMANDER HE WAS WOLSELEY'S EQUAL: OUR ONLY OTHER GENERAL.'

BOBS

There's a little red faced man,
Which is Bobs.
Rides the tallest 'orse 'e can –
Our Bobs.
If it bucks or kicks or rears,
'E can sit for twenty years
With a smile round both 'is ears –
Can't yer, Bobs?

RUDYARD KIPLING
1899

When Kipling at the dawn of the war had sung of 'fifty thousand horse and foot going to Table Bay'; the statement had seemed extreme. Now it was growing on the public mind that four times this number would not be an excessive estimate.

CD

1900	JANUARY	2000
Monday • The enemy round Ladysmith celebrated the New Year and the anniversary of the Jameson Raid with a nocturnal salute – all their guns firing into Ladysmith	**1**	**Saturday**
Tuesday • Reconnaissance made by Buller's Force towards Hlangwane Hill without loss	**2**	**Sunday**

VC

Sir John Milbanke: Lieutenant (later Colonel) 10th Hussars: *Gazetted 6 July 1900*
5 January 1900: Near Colesberg: During a reconnaissance, Lieutenant Milbanke, when retiring under fire, with a small patrol, rode back to help one of his men whose horse was exhausted. Notwithstanding the fact that he was severely wounded in the thigh, the Lieutenant took the man up on his own horse under very heavy fire and got him safely back to camp.

VC

James Masterson: Lieutenant (later Major): 1st Batallion, The Devonshire Regiment: *VC Gazetted 4 June 1901*
6 January 1900: Ladysmith: Wagon Hill: Lieutenant Masterson was commanding one of the three companies of his regiment which captured a position held by the enemy. The companies were then exposed to very heavy fire from the right and left front, so the Lieutenant undertook to get a message to the I.L.H., to fire to the left front in order to check the enemy's fire. To do this he had to cross an open space of 100 yards swept by heavy cross-fire, and although wounded in both thighs, he managed to deliver his message before falling, exhausted.

VC

Robert Scott: Private: 1st Batallion The Manchester Regiment: *VC Gazetted 26 July 1901*
6 January 1900: Ladysmith: Caesar's Camp: During an attack on the hill, 16 men of 'D' Co. were defending one of the slopes. The defenders were under heavy fire all day, the majority being killed and their positions occupied by the enemy. At last only Privates Scott and Pitts remained. They held their post for 15 hours without food or water, all the time exchanging deadly fire with the enemy, until relief troops had retaken the lost ground and pushed the enemy off the hill.

VC

James Pitts: Private (later Corporal): 1st Batallion The Manchester Regiment: *VC Gazetted 26 July 1901*
6 January 1900: Ladysmith: Caesar's Camp: During an attack on the hill, 16 men of 'D' Co. were defending one of the slopes of the hill. The defenders were under heavy fire all day, the majority being killed and their positions occupied by the enemy. At last only Privates Pitts and Scott remained. They held their post for 15 hours without food or water, all the time exchanging deadly fire with the enemy, until relief troops had retaken the lost ground and pushed the enemy off the hill.

The first two posthumous VC's

VC

Robert Digby-Jones: Lieutenant: Corps of Royal Engineers: *VC Gazetted 8 August 1902*
6 January 1900: Ladysmith: During the attack on Wagon Hill, Lieutenant Digby-Jones and Trooper Albrecht of the I.L.H. led the force which re-occupied the top of the hill at a critical moment, just as the three foremost attacking Boers reached it. The leader was shot by Lieutenant Digby-Jones and the other two by Trooper Albrecht. ***Buried Ladysmith Cemetery***

VC

Herman Albrecht: Trooper: Imperial Light Horse: *VC Gazetted 8 August 1902*
6 January 1900: Ladysmith: During the attack on Wagon hill, Lieutenant Digby-Jones, RE, and Trooper Albrecht led the force occupying the hill, at a critical moment, just as the three foremost attacking Boers reached it. The leader was shot by Digby-Jones and the other two by Trooper Albrecht.
Buried Wagon Hill Cemetery

1900	JANUARY	2000
Wednesday • Imperium et Libertas – Empire and Liberty (Motto: I.L.H.)	**3**	**Monday**
Thursday *'Medicines are now at an end and men are dying mainly for want of them.'*	**4**	**Tuesday**
Friday • One VC *'Sun-stroke is becoming frequent, and seems to take advantage of our low-toned condition.'*	**5**	**Wednesday**
Saturday • Five VCs • Battle of Wagon Hill • Major Boer attack on Ladysmith; 17 hours fighting	**6**	**Thursday**
Sunday • Thanksgiving communion service in All Saints Church – George White present • Boers collect their dead: British bury theirs *'Tell England, ye who pass this monument, we who died serving her rest here content: I.L.H.'*	**7**	**Friday**
Monday • British Forces south of Tugela total 30 000 men	**8**	**Saturday**
Tuesday *'Indians tottered and staggered under green-curtained dhoolies.'*	**9**	**Sunday**

Extract from Vol III:

The Selected Works of Mahatma Gandhi

P 107: … Before closing this chapter, I must place a noteworthy incident on record. Among those who were in Ladysmith when it was invested by the Boers, there were besides Englishmen a few stray Indian settlers. Some of these were traders, while the rest were indentured labourers, working on the railways or as servants to English gentlemen, one of whom was Parbhusingh. The officer in command at Ladysmith assigned various duties to every resident of the place. The most dangerous and most responsible work was assigned to Parbhusingh who was a 'coolie'. On a hill near Ladysmith the Boers had stationed a pom-pom (Long Tom), whose operations destroyed many buildings and even occasioned some loss of life. An interval of a minute or two (20 seconds) must pass before a shell which had been fired from the gun reached a distant objective. If the besieged got even such a short notice, they could take cover before the shell dropped in the town and thus save themselves. Parbhusingh was to sit perched up in a tree, all the time that the gun was working, with his eyes fixed on the hill and to ring a bell the moment he observed a flash. On hearing the bell, the residents of Ladysmith instantly took cover and saved themselves from the deadly cannon ball whose approach was thus announced.

The officer in charge of Ladysmith, in eulogizing the invaluable services rendered by Parbhusingh, stated that he worked so zealously that not once had he failed to ring the bell. It need hardly be said that his own life was constantly in peril. The story of his bravery came to be known in Natal and at last reached the ears of Lord Curzon, then Viceroy of India, who sent a Kashmir robe for presentation to Parbhusingh and wrote to the Natal Government, asking them to carry out the presentation ceremony with all possible publicity. This duty was assigned to the Mayor of Durban who held a public meeting in the Town Hall for the purpose. This incident has a twofold lesson for us. First, we should not despise any man, however humble or insignificant-looking he may be. Secondly, no matter how timid a man is, he is capable of the loftiest heroism when he is put to the test.

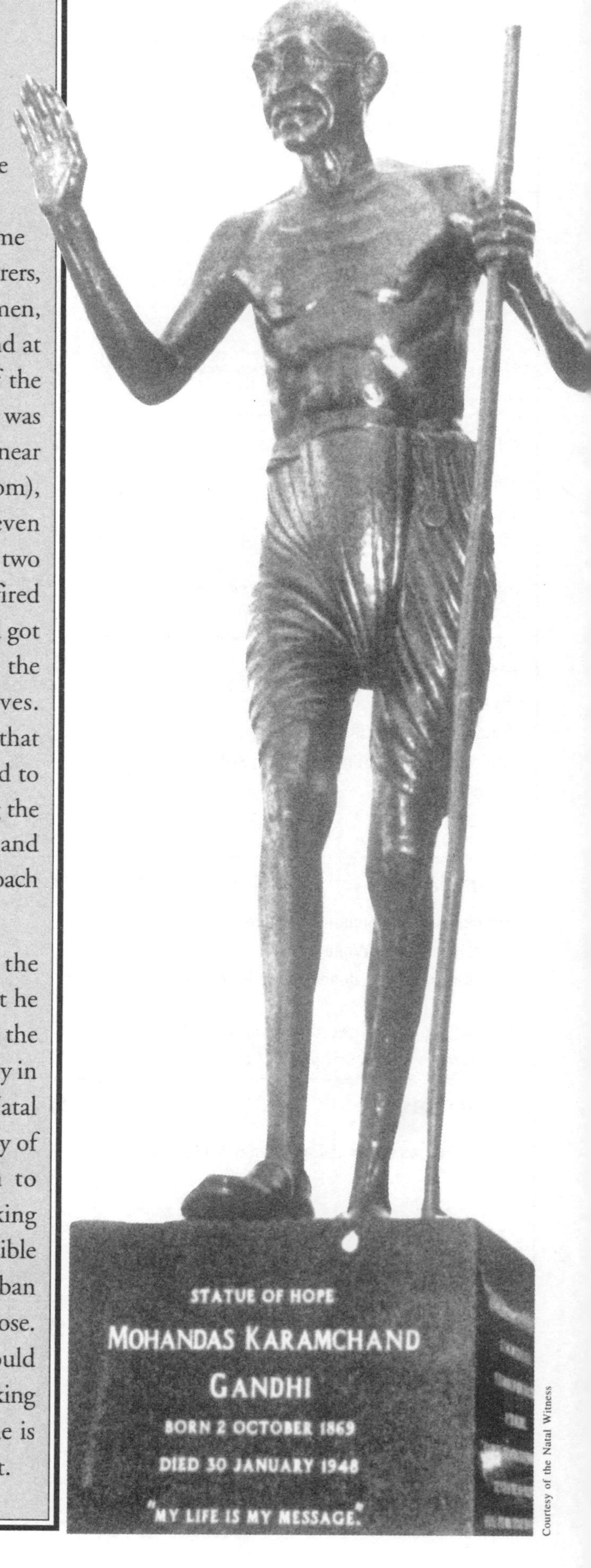

Courtesy of the Natal Witness

1900	JANUARY	2000
Wednesday • Lords Roberts and Kitchener arrive at Cape Town • General Buller moves forward towards Springfield and Dundonald seizes Potgieter's Drift	10	Monday
Thursday • Buller's Force crosses the Tugela at Potgieter's Drift • Death of Earl of Ava	11	Tuesday
Friday *'Far down in the valley the silver Tugela wound, linking hills and mountains: until lost on the right and left of our encampment.'*	12	Wednesday
Saturday • 500 men of the City Imperial Volunteers leave for the Cape	13	Thursday
Sunday *'The effects of my recent illness were still heavy upon me.' – GWS*	14	Friday
Monday • G.W. Steevens succumbs to Enteric: buried 23h30	15	Saturday
Tuesday • Warren moves to Trichardt's Drift	16	Sunday

'ISANDLWANA WAS ONE OF THE WORST DISASTERS TO BE INFLICTED ON ORDINARY SOLDIERS BY THE INCOMPETENCE OF THEIR OFFICERS UNTIL THE FIRST WORLD WAR BROKE ALL RECORDS.' – JP

Isandlwana

SCARLET coats, and crash o' the band,
The grey of a pauper's gown,
A soldier's grave in Zululand,
And a woman in Brecon Town.

My little lad for a soldier boy,
(Mothers o' Brecon Town!)
My eyes for tears and his for joy
When he went from Brecon Town,
His for the flags and the gallant sights
His for the medals and his for the fights,
And mine for the dreary, rainy nights
At home in Brecon Town.

They say he's laid beneath a tree,
(Come back to Brecon Town!)
Shouldn't I know?—I was there to see:
(It's far to Brecon Town!)

It's me that keeps it trim and drest
With a briar there and a rose by his breast—
The English flowers he likes the best
That I bring from Brecon Town.

And I sit beside him—him and me,
(We're back to Brecon Town.)
To talk of the things that used to be
(Grey ghosts of Brecon Town);
I know the look o' the land and sky,
And the bird that builds in the tree near by,
And times I hear the jackals cry,
And me in Brecon Town.

Golden grey on miles of sand
The dawn comes creeping down;
It's day in far off Zululand
And night in Brecon Town.

JOHN MCCRAE
(*IN FLANDERS FIELD* YET TO COME 1914)

This poem, perhaps John McCrae's finest, published in 1910, came from a visit to Brecon in Wales, where he had met a deranged middle-aged woman whose son had been killed at the massacre by the Zulus in 1879.

NOTES:

'Both Melvill and Coghill were cited for gallantry and they would have been recommended to Her Majesty for the VC had they survived. It took more than another twenty years, during the Boer War, to finally make allowances for the posthumous award of the Cross, and the relatives of the two men applied to the War Office to have the question of the dead heroes' awards reopened. King Edward VII refused to grant the crosses. There the matter rested until 1906 when Mrs Melvill addressed a direct petition to the King who finally consented to allow the posthumous award of the VC to six men, one of whom had been dead for nearly sixty years. The London Gazette of 15 January 1907 announced the granting of the VC to the surviving relatives of all six, including the two officers who died together at Isandlwana'.

‘A MISERABLE TALE IS BEST TOLD BADLY.’ – GS

1900	JANUARY	2000
Wednesday • Lord Dundonald, with a mounted force, collides with the Boers west of Acton Homes, and after some fighting, takes the enemy’s kopje • Warren crosses the Tugela	**17**	Monday
Thursday • Churchill takes part in a skirmish in which some twenty Boer prisoners were taken • 8th Division to mobilize at Aldershot *‘Major Childe was soon killed.’*	**18**	Tuesday
Friday • Warren moves up Venter’s Spruit and attacks the Boer right flank	**19**	Wednesday
Saturday • First attempt to storm the Heights: Warren orders an attack on a hill to the left, under cover of an artillery bombardment • 2nd Draught of the City Imperial Volunteers embark for Cape Town	**20**	Thursday
Sunday • The part played by Buller is that of critic rather than commander – full of advice but reluctant to give orders • Message from Ladysmith stating that the place is practically impregnable	**21**	Friday
Monday • Anniversary of Isandlwana and Rorke’s Drift 1879 *‘The heat to-day is awful, and the flies are worse, biting our cuts, eating our meals, and washing themselves in our tea, besides otherwise taking up our attention.’*	**22**	Saturday
Tuesday • Midnight capture of Spioenkop: Boers surprised and flee: British occupy Height	**23**	Sunday

CHILDE’S EPITAPH: ‘IS IT WELL WITH THE CHILD? AND SHE ANSWERED, ‘IT IS WELL.’ – 2 KINGS 4:16

'SPION KOP, PROPERLY USED, WAS THE KEY OF THE POSITION, AND THE KEY THAT WOULD HAVE OPENED THE DOOR TO LADYSMITH.' – JBA

Spioenkop

The Burghers on Spioenkop never exceeded more than 500 men. The British soldiers were unable to deploy because of their large numbers in the limited area on the summit. At dusk the fire ceased and by 10pm Thorneycroft, with his whole force, evacuated the hill. By then most of the burghers had already withdrawn and the battlefield became a desolate scene marked by the moaning and groaning of the wounded.

The manner in which the burghers handled their artillery compensated for their disadvantage in numbers and proved to be the decisive factor. The British on the other hand were unable to make full tactical use of their artillery owing to lack of observation and a failure of communications; their heliograph being shot to pieces.

General Woodgate had been mortally wounded about ten o'clock in the morning; the command came by a natural devolution to Colonel Thorneycroft, and this big, powerful man, certainly the best mark on the hill, moved about fearlessly all day and was untouched.

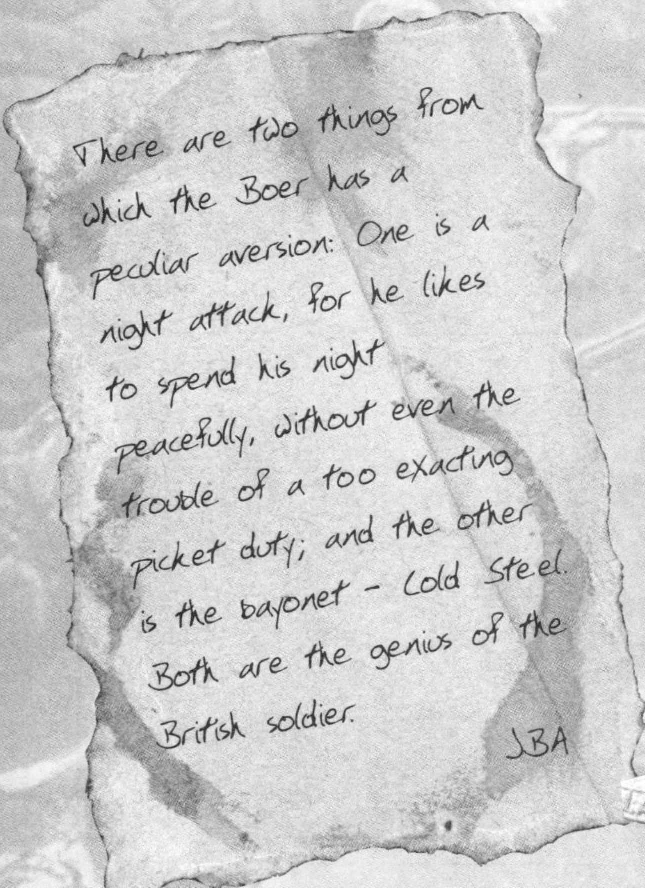
There are two things from which the Boer has a peculiar aversion: One is a night attack, for he likes to spend his night peacefully, without even the trouble of a too exacting picket duty; and the other is the bayonet – Cold Steel. Both are the genius of the British soldier.

JBA

> **Spioenkop:** 'The Boers had three guns playing like hoses on our men. On the west of the hill they were firing a Vickers-Maxim, in the middle a large Creusot gun, on the east of the hill another Vickers-Maxim. It was a triangular fire. Our men on Spion Kop had no gun. When on earth would the artillery come? Guns were the only thing that could make the hill either tenable or useful. When on earth would they come? No sign of them yet, not even a sign of a mountain battery, and we who watched wriggled in our anxiety. The question now was whether enough men could live through the shelling till the guns came.'

'AFTERMATH: NOT THE BRITISH ARMY, BUT THE BRITISH GENERALS: AN ARMY OF LIONS LED BY STAGS, NOT AN ARMY OF STAGS LED BY LIONS.'

1900	JANUARY	2000
Wednesday • Churchill climbs the hill twice; firstly to confirm Thorneycroft's command, and later, to assure Thorneycroft that fresh troops would dig in and hold the position the following day • Battle of Spioenkop – heavy British casualties Both sides abandon hill	**24**	Monday
Thursday • Boers first to re-occupy Spioenkop • Buller commences withdrawal across theTugela	**25**	Tuesday
Friday • British recross the Tugela without any losses • 1 500-odd men had been lost in a week's fighting	**26**	Wednesday
Saturday • Peak of fever cases in Ladysmith – 1 314 Daily death rate averages 8	**27**	Thursday
Sunday • General French arrives at Cape Town to confer with Lord Roberts *'We are again without food for our horses, and there is none to be had for love or money.'*	**28**	Friday
Monday *'Flies are an awful pest, so Nurse Otto has torn up some muslin, and this we use to cover our faces.'*	**29**	Saturday
Tuesday • Hospital ship *Maine* arrives at Durban • Churchill meets his mother and brother	**30**	Sunday

John the Swell

A Poem

(Founded on an incident at the Battle of Spioenkop, 24th, January, 1900)

by Corporal Drake – Scottish Rifles

Was I at the War, Sir? Why yes, see this 'ere scar?
I got that at Spion Kop, sir, – no, we didn't get a bar,
God knows the fight was hard enough – some said t'was worse than hell,
I 'aint been yet to that place, so of course I cannot tell.

Many killed and wounded? Why bless yer, Sir, a lot,
Brave 'uns too. All soldiers to the backbone we had got
Fighting on that hill, Sir, but the bravest one that fell
Was a private in our Regiment, they called him 'John the Swell'.

You know, we soldiers, as a rule, are a rough and ready set,
Some's had a lot of schooling, others, little, you can bet.
But we can do our bit of reading and writing, in a way,
So we understand what's going on, by the papers every day.

But this 'ere chap, I'm speaking of, was a proper mashing bloke –
A chap as never knew what 'twas to go without his toke.
Why, Sir, when he enlisted, he'd collars, ties and cuffs,
And fairly took the biscuit aside of us young roughs.

He wouldn't tell us who he was, and we didn't like to ask,
We could see to try and pump him would be no easy task.
Such a quiet sort of fellow, with a fine good-looking face,
But we soon found out he'd tumbled – that he was out of place.

I suppose we must have worried him with our rough and noisy ways,
And we used to 'cod' him awful, until, one night he says –
'If you interfere with me again, really, 'pon my word
I shall severely thrash you.' But that, Sir, ne'er occurred.

There was something in his eye, Sir, that seemed somehow to say –
'I'll keep my word and don't forget'; so from that very day
We left him to hisself, sir, though sometimes we had to grin,
To see him use a toothpick, while us – a common pin.

When we was ordered out, Sir, the fighting had begun,
And we guessed we'd have to rough it, and have to use the gun,
And we thought that digging trenches, and sleeping out at night,
Would upset 'John, the Swell', sir, and give him quite a fright;

And bless yer, Sir, that chap he marched and worked just like a horse,
And always wore a pleasant look, which made us think, of course,
That we hadn't acted rightly, when we'd sneered at and made fun
Of one worth two of us; and we were sorry every one.

And we tried to make amends, Sir, so we up and asked him straight
If he'd but forget the past, in fact wipe it off the slate.
And bless yer, Sir, he only smiled, and didn't make a fuss,
But murmured something about 'Forgive that trespass against us.'

Well, we'd done a bit of 'roughing it' when the New Year came along
And the boys were more for singing hymns than a noisy comic song.
'Twas the first month in the year, Sir, and on the 24th
When we forded the Tugela, in battle to go forth.

I shall ne'er forget the climbing; the day was broiling hot;
But we got up there somehow, Sir, and saw an awful lot
Of wounded men alying along the dangerous slope,
Some looking with that far-off look that doesn't give much hope.

Yes, we got up to the front, Sir, how, I cannot say,
The Almighty must have helped us all through that trying day.
'Our Captain – such a brave 'un – he led us o'er the brow,
With fixed swords we charged the trenches, I don't recollect quite how.

We managed to get near them through that storm of shot and shell,
And foremost to the front, I noticed 'John, the Swell'.
Then came the worst I ever saw, we were in a perfect hell;
Shrapnell bursting o'er us, and scores of shrieking shell.

Our ranks were getting thin, Sir; our Captain he lay dead,
Still grasping his revolver; shot, right through the head.
I was firing through a loop-hole, behind a lump of rock,
When I felt a sharp pain in the cheek – it gave me quite a shock.

Somehow I must have fainted, for I'd got a nasty hit
From a piece of flying shell, Sir; but I was all right in a bit,
And 'John, the Swell' stood o'er me, and murmured – 'lay quite still;
And bye-and-bye I'll try and get you carried down the hill.'

And I noticed blood was trickling in a stream right down his face;
His left wrist, it was bandaged, but he still stuck to his place,
And when I said – "Why, John, you're hit,' he smiled and said 'all right";
'They're only scratches, Billy'; but his face was awful white.

I begged and prayed – 'Oh get down, mate, you'll surely bleed to death.'
I knew that he was suffering, he could hardly get his breath;
His face was stern, his teeth were set, he answered no reply
But kept his rifle spitting – he meant to do or die.

Till at last he fell right o'er me – it gave me such a fright;
Shot, right through the heart, Sir, I shall ne'er forget the sight.
A peaceful smile upon his face, with rifle still in hand,
His eyes they seemed to say to me, 'I'm in a better land.'

And I cried, Sir, like a baby, it nearly broke my heart
To think, in a place like that, Sir, for ever we should part.
They buried him that evening, in a rough and stony grave,
And someone wrote upon a stone, in big words, 'John, the Brave.'

They took me to the hospital, and I managed to pull round,
And then they sent me home, Sir, and here, I'm safe and sound.
But when I thinks of war, Sir, I gets into a spell
Thinking of the lost ones, especially 'John, the Swell'.

1900	JANUARY	**2000**
Wednesday	**31**	Monday
• Naval Brigade with Grant's Guns lands at Port Elizabeth		

Sound argument or calculated spite?

Comment on Sir Charles Warren's Spioenkop Report to the Chief of Staff 29/01/00:

Spearman's Camp, 20th January 1900.

Secretary of State,
In forwarding this report I am constrained to make the following remarks, not necessarily for publication:-
… 'The days went on. I saw no attempt on the part of General Warren either to grapple with the situation or to command his force himself. By the 23rd I calculated that the enemy, who were about 600 strong on the 16th, were not less than 15 000, and General White confirmed this estimate. We had really lost our chance by Sir C. Warren's slowness. He seems to me a man who can do well what he can do himself, but who cannot command, as he can use neither his staff nor subordinates. I can never employ him again on an independent command.

On the 19th I ought to have assumed command myself; I saw that things were not going well – indeed, everyone saw that. I blame myself now for not having done so. I did not, because I thought that if I did I should discredit General Warren in the estimation of the troops, and that if I were shot, and he had to withdraw across the Tugela, and they had lost confidence in him, the consequences might be very serious.

I must leave it to higher authority whether this argument was a sound one. Anyway, I feel convinced that we had a good chance on the 17th, and that we lost it.'

REDVERS BULLER, General

Buller: He could scarcely conceal his satisfaction at the turn of events, and on arrival at Warren's Headquarters briskly dismissed any suggestion that the action might be resumed
Leo Amery

Beyond stating the fact that on five different occasions during the ensuing three months Warren was given an independent command by Buller (one of the five being that on which he was placed in command of the whole of the troops north of the Tugela from February 24th until the relief of Ladysmith on March 1st), but that almost without exception the name of Warren was omitted from the despatches on these operations, it must be left to the reader to decide how far this criticism is either just or true.
WW

Of Buller's three despatches of January 30th, 1900, Warren did not see the first two until after he had left Natal in April, while he was entirely unaware of the existence of the third until its publication in 1902. WW

Similarity: Majuba

History repeats itself: The war of 1881 bears a good deal of similarity to recent events. I quote from a history of the Transvaal:

'War broke out on December 13, 1880. The English population, which, depending on the promises of the government, had flocked into the country, were beleaguered in different towns, and a small force under Colonel Anstruther was almost annihilated at Bronkhorst Spruit. It was, however, on colonial territory that our most humiliating defeats were experienced. General Sir George Colley, then Governor of Natal, and Commander-in-Chief of the Forces, marched to the relief of the beleaguered town with a small army of 1 000 men. His progress was arrested by a Boer commando under Joubert. On attempting to force the passage at Laing's Nek on the 28th of January, 1881, Colley was driven back to his camp on Mount Prospect with heavy loss. On the 7th of February another crushing reverse was experienced on the Ingogo Heights. After a fortnight's delay, during which reinforcements arrived, Colley, with 600 men, executed that amazing ascent of Majuba Hill. His position was attacked at dawn, on the 27th of February, by a small party of Boers; and nearly half the British force, which ran short of ammunition, were killed or wounded in the panic which ensued.

... 'Colley, whatever his capabilities as a general may have been, met his death like a soldier whilst endeavouring to bring his men to the charge. Only one of the Boers was killed; their loss in the three engagements barely exceeding a dozen men. We can well understand that their predicament, in his thanksgiving sermon, should take for his text: *The sword of the Lord and of Gideon.*

'This action practically closed the war, and the reinforcements which arrived were never used. Peace was concluded as soon as possible, and the Government of the South African Republic was again formally recognised.'

WK-LD

His Gallantry on 'Shameful Hill'

To you, who know the force of war,
You, that for England wander far,
You, that have seen the Ghazis fly
From English lads not born to die;
You, that have lain where, deadly chill,
The mist crept o'er the Shameful Hill;
You that have conquered, mile by mile,
The currents of unfriendly Nile,
And cheered the March, and eased the strain
When politics made valour vain,
Ian, to you, from banks of Ken,
We send our lays of Englishmen!

Andrew Lang: Hamilton on Majuba

Ah, horrible war, amazing medley of the glorious and the squalid, the pitiful and the sublime, if modern men of light and leading saw your face closer, simple folk would see it hardly ever.

WSCh

1900	**FEBRUARY**	**2000**
Thursday *'For it is dull work fighting week after week without alcohol or green vegetables.' – WSCh*	**1**	Tuesday
Friday • 'Chevril' horse extract issued in Ladysmith • Bread rations ½lb daily	**2**	Wednesday
Saturday *'History repeats itself.'*	**3**	Thursday
Sunday *'The war of 1881 bears a good deal of similarity to recent events.'*	**4**	Friday
Monday • Buller starts third attempt to relieve Ladysmith via Vaalkrantz	**5**	Saturday
Tuesday • Lord Roberts leaves Cape Town for Modder River	**6**	Sunday

Sir Redvers Buller

'Tragically, however, the Redvers Buller of the S A War was not made of bronze, but of plaster, the powers of strong leadership and lightning decision gone, together with the lust to kill, to risk everything in battle. Behind the still impressive exterior were wavering weakness, hesitation, an inclination for safety first. But still worse, he had developed what might be noble in the pacifist but what was fatal in the soldier – a fatherly compassion for the thousands of men he commanded. He had always been a tough disciplinarian but nevertheless he had loved his men as deeply as they loved him. But now his love had become reinforced by an extreme protectiveness which in war was an absurdity … The mind of this officer whose thinking had once been consistently positive, now tossed on waves of alternating optimism and pessimism. Of course he had reasons for this agonising uncertainty. The civilian armies of Kruger, many fighting in their Dutch civilian frock-coats, were putting Great Britain to shame and all Europe was laughing at her failures.'

ALDERSHOT REVIEW: JOHN WALTERS

Intombi Graves: 8 Feb: I saw the natives digging trenches, for by this time the death-rate has become very heavy. At first separate graves were dug and an iron cross put over each. On these I read names from nearly every regiment in Ladysmith, and noticed that about twenty of the men of HMS Powerful are buried there. Every day we see young fellows who have passed away carried out in their blankets. They are then buried the same day. Seldom a day passed when fewer than five to twenty-five are added to the number of dead. Their bodies are then taken to a covered-in place, the blanket is sewn up, and a card stating name, age, and religion attached.

Buller: The Ferryman of the Tugela

'Our generals', remarked Asquith, the future prime minister, after reading one of Buller's dispatches, 'seem neither able to win victories nor to give convincing reasons for their defeats.'

Buller had lost his nerve. He was one of those unfortunate soldiers who are competent subordinates but fail in novel situations when in high command.

1900	FEBRUARY	2000
Wednesday • Repaired Long Tom, alias The Jew, starts bombarding Kimberley • Vaalkrantz evacuated – British withdraw to Frere base camp	**7**	Monday
Thursday • Another general retirement – The Churchill brothers watched the fighting from the nearside of the river • Lord Roberts reaches Modder River	**8**	Tuesday
Friday • George Labram killed at Kimberley by a shell from Short Tom	**9**	Wednesday
Saturday • Buller and his main army return to Frere	**10**	Thursday
Sunday • In two months of fighting, Buller had involved his troops in a series of bungled battles • Lord Roberts' great flank march begins	**11**	Friday
Monday • Churchill was unaffected by the prevailing gloom: Both brothers included in a cavalry contingent to reconnoitre the line of advance to Hussar Hill • Boers commence attempt to dam the Klip River near Intombi camp	**12**	Saturday
Tuesday • Jack Churchill, hit in the leg, is packed off to Durban and taken on board the *Maine* to be nursed by his mother *'Enteric: this insidious and awful fever.'*	**13**	Sunday

'EXPERIENCE ALSO SHOWED THAT WAR WAS TOO SERIOUS A MATTER TO BE LEFT TO STATESMEN.'

Kimberley Relieved

Rhodes, who stood for the future of South Africa as clearly as the Dopper Boer stood for its past, had, both in features and in character, some traits which may, without extravagance, be called Napoleonic

JBA

The scheming Cecil Rhodes, bent on creating a British hegemony from Cairo to the Cape, sought to exploit the discontent of the Uitlanders and sent his crony Jameson, with a bunch of hired thugs, to provoke them into an armed uprising. This conspiracy was a total failure but it united the Boers behind their President, the stern Paul Kruger, and against the British. Always connoisseurs of good firearms, they began to buy large numbers of excellent Mauser rifles and Herr Krupp's Quick-Firing Field Guns from the Germans.

The British Governor in Cape Town, Sir Alfred Milner, backed by the Colonial Secretary, Joseph Chamberlain, adopted an intransigent attitude towards Afrikaner ambitions for independence and maintained the principle of British suzerainty over the Transvaal and the Orange Free State. In October 1899 troops arrived from India to reinforce the small Imperial force already in South Africa, and Milner issued an ultimatum to President Kruger. But it was the Boers who struck first. In a series of rapid manoeuvres they invaded Natal and Cape Colony and laid siege to Mafeking, Kimberley and Ladysmith. The war which followed was long, bitter and almost completely pointless, since the Boers achieved their self-government within eight years of the ending of hostilities. The scorched-earth policy, introduced by Roberts and followed through by Kitchener, and the confinement of Boer women and children, as well as thousands of farm labourers, in concentration camps, where thousands died, left a legacy of bitterness which accounts in part for the intransigence of Afrikaner attitudes to this day.

VC

Francis Parsons: Lieutenant 1st Batallion: The Essex Regiment: *Gazetted 20 Nov 1900*
18 February 1900: Paardeberg: A private was wounded and, while trying to take cover, was wounded again. Lieutenant Parsons went to his assistance, dressed his wounds under heavy fire, fetched water from the river nearby, still under heavy fire, and then carried him to a place of safety. The Lieutenant was killed in action a short time later.

VC awarded posthumously

VC

Alfred Atkinson: Sergeant: 1st Batallion: The Yorkshire Regiment: *Gazetted 8 Aug 1902*
18 Feb 1900: During the Battle of Paardeberg, Sergeant Atkinson went out seven times under heavy fire to obtain water for the wounded. At the seventh attempt he was wounded in the head and died a few days afterwards.

'THESE BOERS MIGHT BE BRUTAL, MIGHT BE TREACHEROUS; BUT THEY HELD THEIR HEADS LIKE GENTLEMEN. TOMMY AND THE VELD PEASANT – A COMEDY OF GOOD MANNERS IN WET AND COLD AND MUD AND BLOOD!' – GS

1900	FEBRUARY	2000
Wednesday • Fourth attempt to relieve Ladysmith: Dundonald seizes Hussar Hill, Colenso	**14**	Monday
Thursday • Kimberley relieved • General John French and Major Haig meet Cecil Rhodes	**15**	Tuesday
Friday • Cronje evacuates position at Magersfontein • Capture of Cingolo Hill east of Hlangwane, running north west to the Tugela	**16**	Wednesday
Saturday • Cronje stopped at Paardeberg • Buller attacks Monte Cristo	**17**	Thursday
Sunday • Two VC's • Lyttelton captures Monte Cristo • Battle of Paardeberg – Cronje surrounded	**18**	Friday
Monday • Churchill watches the action from Hlangwane Hill • Buller takes Hlangwane Hill • Lord Roberts arrives at Paardeberg	**19**	Saturday
Tuesday • Cronje's laager bombarded – De Wet attempts to relieve Cronje • Colenso occupied – Boers withdraw to northern bank of Tugela	**20**	Sunday

'SOLITARY TREES, IF THEY GROW AT ALL, GROW STRONG.' – WSCH

The Battle of Pieters:

The Tugela seemed to be ten thousand times in flood;
Never before had it such a mighty rushing voice.

All the maxims the battalions had between them were
Firing too till the water round the barrels boiled and boiled again;

The colts added their deep, deliberate rapping;
And the river, drawing it all down, gave an impressive
resonance to the continuous sweeping roar.

It was February 27, and the hills east of Railway Hill
Were being prepared for victorious attack

JBA

Albert Curtis: Private (later Sergeant): 2nd Batallion: The East Surrey Regiment:
VC Gazetted 15 January 1901
23 February 1900: Onderbrook Spruit, Colenso: A Colonel lay all day in an open space under close fire from the enemy who fired on any man who moved. The Colonel was wounded eight or nine times. Private Curtis after several attempts, managed to reach him, bound his wounds and gave him his own flask, all under heavy fire. He then, with the assistance of another man, tried to move the wounded officer who, fearing that both men would be killed, told them to leave him. This they refused to do, and eventually managed to carry him to safety.

James Firth: Sergeant: 1st Batallion: The Duke of Wellington's Regiment:
VC Gazetted 11 June 1901
24 Feb 1900: Plewman's farm, near Arundel, CC: Sergeant Firth picked up and carried to cover a Lance-Corporal who was lying wounded and exposed to heavy fire. Later in the day, when the enemy had advanced to within a short distance of the firing line, Sergeant Firth rescued a Second Lieutenant who was dangerously wounded, and carried him over the crest of a ridge to safety. He himself was shot through the nose and eye while doing so.

Edgar Inkson: Lieutenant (later Colonel) RAMC, attd The Royal Inniskilling Fusiliers:
VC Gazetted 15 Jan 1901
24 February 1900: Hart's Hill, Colenso: Lieutenant Inkson carried a young officer, who was severely wounded and unable to walk, for three or four hundred yards, under very heavy fire, to a place of safety.

Conwyn Mansel-Jones: Captain: The West Yorkshire Regiment: *VC Gazetted 27 July 1900*
27 February 1900: Tugela Heights: Colenso: The companies of The West Yorkshire Regiment met with severe shell and rifle fire on the northern slope of Terrace Hill and their advance was temporarily checked. Captain Mansel-Jones, however, by his strong initiative and example, restored confidence and in spite of his falling very seriously wounded, the men took the whole ridge without further check.

1900	FEBRUARY	2000
Wednesday • Warren's 5th Division advances across the Tugela • Kitchener's Kopje captured • Roberts offers safe conduct for women and children in Cronje's Laager – Refused	**21**	Monday
Thursday • Buller occupies Wynne Hills – Attack on Boer positions lasts three days • Ladysmith bread ration increased to 1lb per day	**22**	Tuesday
Friday • One VC • Buller unsuccessfully attacks Inniskilling Hill – heavy losses on both sides. • The cordon around Cronje tightens – Boers from Natal beaten off	**23**	Wednesday
Saturday • Two VCs • Heavy shell-fire from Boers on Grobler's Kloof very effective	**24**	Thursday
Sunday • The bloody stalemate lasts four days • Armistice for the removal of wounded and burial of the dead at Tugela Heights	**25**	Friday
Monday • Finding the Langewachte Spruit commanded by strong entrenchments, Buller sends his guns and baggage back to the south bank of the Tugela and looks for a new crossing	**26**	Saturday
Tuesday • One VC • Anniversary of Majuba (1881). Surrender of Cronje and 4 000 Boers at Paardeberg • Battle of Pieter's Hill – Boers beat a hasty retreat	**27**	Sunday

Relief of Ladysmith

Gaunt men greeted one with wisps of
Smiles without violence of feeling,
Gaunt grooms combed gaunt artillery horses
With the husks of the old assiduity.
As for the garrison 'cutting their way out',
In the exhilarating phrase,
There was not a company of infantry
That could march a mile and a half,
And not a horse that could pull a gun
Three miles without dropping.

The garrison were a little inclined to be angry with us for having taken so long to reach them.
JBA

Beginning of Siege	Termination
+ 5 000 horses	2 907 horses
+ 4 500 mules	3 713 mules
1 700 oxen	252 oxen

Total admissions to Intombi Hospital: 10 688
deaths: 600

Chevril:'It has now become expedient to supplement the fresh meat ration with horseflesh. The better conditioned of the recently emancipated troop-horses were requisitioned. Some had already made their way to the enemy's lines; those that remained by degrees came under the butcher's knife. From this period until the end of the siege, on an average, sixty horses were slaughtered daily for distribution as rations. Considerable ingenuity was displayed by Lieutenant McNalty A.S.C., Captain Young, R.E. and their assistant, Mr Turner, in issuing horsemeat in a palatable form. It was converted into a paste called CHEVRIL, which made a nourishing soup. Sausages and forced meats were also made, and jellies and extracts were manufactured for use in hospitals.'

'LADYSMITH: FAMOUS TO THE UTTERMOST ENDS OF THE EARTH: THE CENTRE OF THE WORLD'S ATTENTION; THE SCENE OF FAMOUS DEEDS; THE CAUSE OF MIGHTY EFFORTS.' – WSCH

1900	FEBRUARY	2000
Wednesday • Lord Dundonald's Flying Column enters Ladysmith – Ladysmith relieved	**28**	**Monday**
Why 1900 was not a Leap Year **Every year that is exactly divisible by 4 is a leap year, except for the years that are exactly divisible by 100. These centurial years are leap years only if they are divisible by 400. As a result, the year 2000 is a leap year, whereas 1900 and 2100 are not leap years.** – The Explanatory Supplement to the Astronomical Almanac, 1992.	**29**	**Tuesday**

THE RELIEF OF LADYSMITH

The following was published after the relief:

To General Buller:

Ladysmith ours?
Now praised be the powers!
Here's to you, Buller, my heart and my hand!
Bells rouse the people,
And flags from each steeple
Flutter to utter the joy of the land.

Thrice unprevailing,
With courage unfailing,
Doggedly British, you still dared the deed,
Knowing what faced you,
You knew how we placed you,
Valiant and gallant to help at our need.

Thanks like a fountain
Shall flow; for each mountain
Flame-girt and steel-girt in anger arose,
Ridge to ridge yielding
More desperate shielding,
All the ground – trench and mount – packed with the foes.

Not that for mothers,
For sisters, for brothers,
You fought incessantly twelve fighting days,
But that you played the game
True to our ancient name,
Buller! ne'er fuller was Britain of praise.
Ladysmith ours?

Fly flags from all towers!
Half-mast were better! we think of the dead;
They who, at Freedom's gate
Thundered and met their fate,
We owe them, we crown them, the heroes you led.

H.D. RAWNSLEY

'LADYSMITH, AT LAST!' – WSCH

'LET IT BE ACKNOWLEDGED THAT BULLER'S WAS THE HARDEST PROBLEM OF THE WAR, AND THAT HE SOLVED IT.' – CD

Official Ceremony

Relief at last … 'About six I had driven out (being still enfeebled with fever) to King's post, to see the tail-end of the Boer waggons disappear. On returning I found all the world running for all they were worth to the lower end of the High-street and shouting wildly. The cause was soon evident. Riding up just past the Anglican Church came a squadron of mounted infantry. They were not our own. Their horses were much too good, and they looked strange. Behind them came another and another. They had crossed the drift that leads to the road along the foot of Caesar's Camp past Intombi to Pieter's and Colenso. There was no mistake about it. They were the advance of the relief column, and more were coming behind. It was Lord Dundonald's Irregulars – Imperial Light Horse, Natal Carbineers, Natal Police, and Border Mounted Rifles.

The road was crammed on both sides with cheering and yelling crowds – soldiers off duty, officers, townspeople, Blacks and Indians, all one turmoil of excitement and joy. By the post office General White met them, and by common consent there was a pause. Most of his Staff were with him too. In a very few words he welcomed the first visible evidence of relief. He thanked his own garrison for their splendid service in the defence, and added that now he would never have to cut down their rations again, a thing that always went to his heart.

Then followed roar after roar of cheering – cheers for White, for Buller, for Ward, for many others. Then, all of a sudden, we found ourselves shouting the National Anthem in every possible key and pitch. Then more cheering and more again.

But it was getting dark. The General and Staff turned towards Headquarters. The new arrivals had to be settled in their quarters for the night. Most were taken in by the Imperial Light Horse – alas! there is plenty of room in their camp now! To right and left the squadrons wheeled, amid greetings and laughter and endless delight. By eight o'clock the street was almost clear, and there was nothing to show how great a change had befallen us.

About ten a tremendous explosion far away told that the Boers were blowing up the bridges behind them as they fled.

And so with to-night the long siege really ends. It is hardly credible yet. For 118 days we have been cut off from the world. All that time we have been more or less under fire, sometimes under terrible fire. What it will be to mix with the great world again and live each day in comparative security we can hardly imagine at present. But the peculiar episode called the Siege of Ladysmith is over.'

– **NEVINSON**

'During most of the forenoon I stood alongside and conversed with a young man of somewhat untidy appearance, in so far as his uniform was concerned. He wore the slouch hat with Sakabula feathers, and badge of the South African Light Horse, to which Regiment he told me he was attached. He asked me my name and then told me he was Winston Churchill, and that he was a War Correspondent attached to the South African Light Horse. I asked him if he was a son of the then stormy petrel in Britain's politics, Lord Randolph Churchill. He replied in the affirmative. How could I know then that I had met and conversed with a man destined to become Britain's most famous and illustrious war time Prime Minister?'

B W MARTIN

Delayed post: At Ladysmith I ascertained that over twenty tons of letters were in the town in less than three days after the Relief … brought in on twelve ox-wagons and two mule-wagons heavily loaded.

4 March: With Ladysmith relieved and reported, Churchill hurried down to Durban to spend a few days with his mother before the *Maine* sailed back to England

'THE DUTCH TONGUE SOUNDS LIKE GERMAN SPOKEN BY PEOPLE WHO WILL NOT TAKE THE TROUBLE TO FINISH PRONOUNCING IT.' – GS

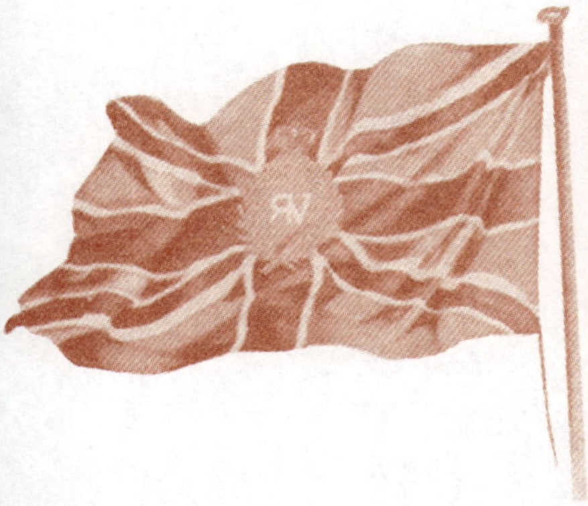

The Homecoming

The flags unfurl! Beat loud the drums!
Shout out the victor's song!
At last the day of truimph comes
For which we've waited long.
Yet while o'erhead bright garlands wave,
And fragrant roses rain,
Forget we not those heroes brave
Who'll ne;er come home again

Bombshell Poem

1900	MARCH	2000
Thursday • Buller visits Ladysmith, having moved his HQ to Nelthorpe • Roberts and Kitchener visit Kimberley and attend a meeting in the town hall	1	Wednesday
Friday • Wagon loads of supplies enter Ladysmith – 11 containing hospital comforts • Cronje and his staff are sent to Simonstown under guard of the City Imperial Volunteers, and put on board HMS *Doris* set to sail to St Helena	2	Thursday
Saturday • Ceremonial entry of relief forces into Ladysmith • Clements advances from Colesberg	3	Friday
Sunday • Labuschagne's Nek captured by Colonial Division under Brabant • Intense heat – fortunately nothing is to happen for a day or two	4	Saturday
Monday • Boer overtures of peace to British Government: Gatacre occupies Stormberg	5	Sunday

'WHAT NEWS? WHAT NEWS? WHAT ANXIOUS ONES ARE WAITING FAR OFF TO KNOW IF US ALL IS WELL!'

The sad experience we had gained from six months' warfare, and more especially the great misfortune that had overtaken the big waggon-camp of General Cronje, were our reasons for a new regulation:

This council also enacted that officers should be very chary in accepting doctors' certificates. The old law had laid it down that if a burgher produced a medical certificate, declaring him unfit for duty, he should be exempted from service. That there had been a grave abuse of this was the experience of almost every officer. There were several very dubious cases; and it was curious to note how many sudden attacks of heart disease occurred – if one were to credit the medical certificates. I remember myself that on the 7th March, when the burghers fled from Poplar Grove, I had thrust upon me suddenly eight separate certificates, which had all been issued that morning, each declaring that some burgher or other was suffering from disease of the heart. When the eighth was presented to me, and I found that it also alleged the same complaint, I lost all patience, and let the doctor know that was quite enough for one day. When this question of certificates was discussed at the council, I suggested in joke that no certificate should be accepted unless it was signed by three old women, as a guarantee of good faith. The system had indeed been carried to such lengths, and certificates had been issued right and left in such lavish manner, that one almost suspected that the English must have had a hand in it!

CdW

NOTES:

In March 1893, Churchill made an unorthodox dash for the Afghan Border, and, on arrival at Peshawar, with the help of a new friend, Captain Aylmer Haldane, was able to get himself appointed as an extra orderly on the staff of the Commander-in-Chief.

1900	MARCH	2000
Tuesday • Colonel Adye repulsed at Houwater • Carnarvon occupied by Colonel Parsons • Natal reported by Sir Redvers Buller to be clear of the enemy	**6**	Monday
Wednesday • Battle of Poplar Grove – becomes Roberts HQ • Gatacre occupies Burghersdorp	**7**	Tuesday
Thursday • Clements occupies Norval's Pont • Brabant occupies Jamestown • Sir Walter Hely Hutchinson, Governor of Natal, visits Ladysmith	**8**	Wednesday
Friday • General Sir George White leaves Ladysmith	**9**	Thursday
Saturday • Battle of Driefontein, 15 miles east of Poplar Grove – Boers flee after dark	**10**	Friday
Sunday • Lord Salisbury replies to Boer peace overtures – British Government refuses	**11**	Saturday
Monday • Lord Roberts continues his march on Bloemfontein unopposed	**12**	Sunday

VC

Henry Engleheart: Sergeant (later Quarter Master-Sergeant): 10th Hussars
Gazetted 5 Oct 1900
13 March 1900: North of Bloemfontein: The party which had destroyed the railway had to get over four deep spruits in order to make their way back through enemy lines. At the fourth spruit the horse of one of the sappers failed to get up the bank and he was left in a very dangerous position. In the face of very heavy fire Sergeant Engleheart went to the rescue of the sapper and his horse. Shortly before this he had shown great gallantry in dashing into the first spruit and dealing with the Boers there, before they had time to rally.

Major-General Sir C.F. Clery K C B

In command of the Second Division in Natal since October 1899, with local rank of Lieutenant-General. He entered the army in 1858; was Professor of Tactics at Sandhurst 1872-5; Deputy-Assistant-Adjutant General in Ireland 1875-7; and at Aldershot 1877-8; was Chief Staff Officer in the Zulu War 1878-9; Brigade-Major at Alexandria in the Egyptian War 1882; Assistant-Adjutant-General in the Sudan Expedition 1884; Deputy-Adjutant and Quarter-Master-General in the Nile Expedition 1884-5; Chief-of-Staff in Egypt 1886-8; and Commandant of the Staff College 1888-93. He commanded the 3rd Infantry Brigade at Aldershot 1895-6, and was Deputy-Adjutant-General to the Forces from 1896 until he left for Africa.

More elaborate and less accurate 'Wanteds' have been published:

'Who is this Clery?' said a newcomer.
'It's General Clery, said a comrade;
'Don't yer know him?'
'No, what's he like?'
'Oh, you can't mistake him at all. Thin, queer-looking bloke, with a puzzle beard and blue whiskers.'

WISE THINKING:

On both sides many men died from head wounds. A favourite method was for a rifleman to fire at a slanting rock in the hope of killing the man behind by a deflected bullet.

– Dr John Clark

To get rid of mosquitoes. These pests prefer beef blood better than they do anything that flows in the veins of human kind. Just put a couple of pieces on plates near your bed at night, and you sleep untroubled by these pests. In the morning you will find them full and stupid, and the meat sucked as dry as an ordinary Railway Hotel customer. Fresh beef, well suited for the purpose, can be obtained at the ration shop, free to residents only.

GW Lines

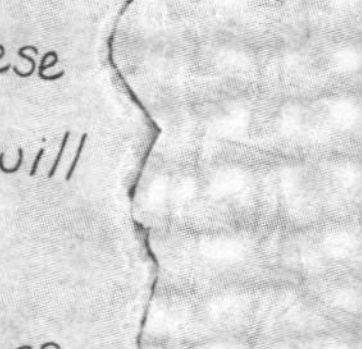

1900	MARCH	2000
Tuesday • One VC • Lord Roberts presented with the keys to Bloemfontein within two miles of the public offices • British flag hoisted over the presidency	**13**	**Monday**
Wednesday • Captain Percy Scott relinquishes his duties as Commandant of Durban	**14**	**Tuesday**
Thursday • Lord Roberts issues a proclamation to the Boers	**15**	**Wednesday**
Friday • Gatacre reaches Springfontein	**16**	**Thursday**
Saturday • Boer Council of War at Kroonstad	**17**	**Friday**
Sunday • Lord Kitchener occupies Prieska • Boers blow up railway bridge at Glen Siding	**18**	**Saturday**
Monday • Rouxville occupied by Major Cumming	**19**	**Sunday**

JOHN FRENCH: 'HAD ESTABLISHED HIMSELF AS BRILLIANT BUT ERRATIC, WITH TWO GREAT SUCCESSES AND TWO CRASS FAILURES TO HIS CREDIT.'

Major-General John D.P. French

Born in 1852. Served in the Militia, but joined the 8th Hussars as Lieutenant in February 1874, and changed to the 19th Hussars in March. Captain 1880; Major 1883. Served in the Nile Expedition in 1884-5, and accompanied Sir H. Stewart's column in an attempt to rescue Gordon at Khartoum. Lieutenant-Colonel, 1885; Colonel, 1889. In command of Cavalry Division in South Africa with rank of Lieutenant-General, 1899; won the victory of Elandslaagte. Major-General 1900 in recognition of his services in relieving Kimberley. John French was to lead the British Expeditionary Forces in France 1914.

Major-General Sir Edward Woodgate

K.C.M.G., C.B., died at Mooi River Hospital, Natal, on the evening of 23 March. He was dangerously wounded in his forehead by a shell at Spion Kop 24 January, when in command of the Lancashire Brigade under Sir Charles Warren, and his recovery was hardly expected at that time. But, after an operation by Dr Frederick Treves, and his subsequent removal to Mooi River, he appeared to improve, and his friends and relations considered him to be so far out of danger that they were expecting him home in the summer. However, it appears that paralysis suddenly supervened towards the end of last week, and the gallant officer gradually sank.

THE ARMY & NAVY GAZETTE MARCH 1900

Edward Robert Prevost Woodgate, C.B., C.M.G., was a son of the Rector of Belbroughton, Worcestershire. Born 1845; entered the Army as ensign in the 4th (King's Own Royal Lancaster) regiment in 1865; served with the Abyssinian Expedition against King Theodore, 1868; in the Ashanti War of 1873-74; on the staff in the Zulu War of 1878-9, when he obtained the Brevet of Major; served as staff officer in the West Indies, 1880-5, and as regimental officer in India, 1885-89; promoted Lieutenant-Colonel, 1893; C.B. 1896; and Colonel, 1897; appointed to command the Regimental District of the King's Own at Lancaster, September, 1897; raised the West African Frontier Regiment in Sierra Leone, and suppressed the native rebellion, 1898-9; invalided home and made C.M.G., and given command of Leicestershire district. In December, 1899, he was appointed to the command of the Ninth Brigade in South Africa; he led the assault on Spion Kop, and was mortally wounded while defending the position gained upon that hill, January 24, 1900.

Sir E.R.P. Woodgate, a competent soldier who was, unfortunately hamstrung by a strong premonition of his impending death in action.

Churchill's third book, *London to Ladysmith via Pretoria*, (completed in March), compiled from his despatches to the *Morning Post*, had been published with astonishing speed. Sent to England, it was in the bookshops by early May.

1900	MARCH	2000
Tuesday • Thaba'Nchu occupied by French	**20**	Monday
Wednesday • Pilcher occupies Leeuw River Mills	**21**	Tuesday
Thursday • Clements occupies Phillippolis • Portuguese Govt sanction passage of troops and stores via Beira	**22**	Wednesday
Friday • Martial law extended to Gordonia • Major-General Sir E.R.P. Woodgate dies at Mooi River	**23**	Thursday
Saturday • 4th New Zealand contingent sails for South Africa • 'C' Battery Royal Canadian Artillery disembark at Beira • Carrington leaves Beira for Marandellas	**24**	Friday
Sunday • Cavalry reconnaissance towards Brandfort	**25**	Saturday
Monday • Pilcher enters Ladybrand • French returns to Bloemfontein	**26**	Sunday

VC

Redvers Buller: Brevet Lieutenant (later General/Sir): 60th Rifles (later The King's Royal Rifle Corps)
Gazetted 17 June 1879
28 March 1879: Hlobane: Zulu War: During the retreat, Lieutenant Colonel Buller, while being hotly pursued by Zulus, rescued a captain of the Frontier Light Horse and carried him on his own horse until he overtook the rearguard. On the same day, under the same circumstances, he carried a lieutenant, whose horse had been killed under him, to a place of safety. Again, on the same day, he saved a trooper whose horse was exhausted, and who would otherwise have been killed by the Zulus who were within 80 yards of him.

VC

Edmund Phipps-Hornby: Major (later Brigadier General): 'Q' Battery Royal Horse Artillery
Gazetted 26 June 1900
31 March 1900: Korn Spruit: Two batteries of the RHA were ambushed with the loss of most of the baggage column and five guns of the leading battery. When the alarm was given, 'Q' Battery, commanded by Major Phipps-Hornby, went into action 1150 yards from the spruit, until the order to retire was received, when the major commanded that the guns and their limbers be run back by hand to a safe place – a most exhausting operation over a considerable distance, but at last all but one of the guns and one limber had been moved to safety and the battery reformed.

VC

Francis Maxwell: Lieutenant (later Brigadier-General): Indian Staff Corps attd Robert's Light Horse
Gazetted 8 March 1901
31 March 1900: Korn Spruit: Lieutenant Maxwell carried out the self-imposed duty of saving the guns. He went out on five different occasions and helped to bring in two guns and three limbers, one of which he, another officer and some gunners dragged in by hand. He also went out with two other officers and tried to get the last gun in and remained there until the attempt had to be abandoned. During a previous campaign, Chitral Expedition, (1895) he had removed the body of a Lieutenant-Colonel of the Corps of Guides, under fire.

VC

Isaac Lodge: Gunner (later Bombadier) 'Q' Battery Royal Horse Artillery
Gazetted 26 June 1900
31 March 1900: Korn Spruit: Two batteries of the RHA were ambushed with the loss of most of the baggage column and five guns of the leading battery. When the alarm was given, 'Q' Battery went into action 1150 yds from the spruit, until the order to retire was received, when the major commanding the battery ordered the guns and their limbers to be run back by hand to a safe place. This most exhausting operation was carried out by, among others, Gunner Lodge, a sergeant and a driver and when at last all but one of the guns and one limber had been moved to safety, the battery was reformed.

VC

Charles Parker: Sergeant: 'Q" Battery, Royal Horse Artillery
Gazetted 26 June 1900
31 March 1900: Korn Spruit: Two batteries of the RHA were ambushed with the loss of most of the baggage column and five guns of the leading battery. When the alarm was given, 'Q' Battery went into action 1150 yards from the spruit, until the order to retire was received, when the major commanding the battery ordered the guns and their limbers to be run back by hand to a safe place. This most exhausting operation was carried out by, among others, Sergeant Parker, a gunner and a driver, and when at last all but one of the guns and one limber had been moved to safety, the battery was reformed. (Award by ballot)

VC

Horace Glasock: Driver: 'Q" Battery, Royal Horse Artillery
Gazetted 26 June 1900
31 March 1900: Korn Spruit: Two batteries of the RHA were ambushed with the loss of most of the baggage column and five guns of the leading battery. When the alarm was given, 'Q' Battery went into action 1150 yards from the spruit, until the order to retire was received, when the major commanding the battery ordered the guns and their limbers to be run back by hand to a safe place. This most exhausting operation was carried out by, among others, Driver Glasock, a gunner and a seargeant, and when at last all but one of the guns and one limber had been moved to safety, the battery was reformed. (Awarded by ballot: Phipps-Hornby, Parker and Lodge)

1900	MARCH	2000
Tuesday • Death of General Piet Joubert: Louis Botha to succeed him • Clements occupies Fauresmith	**27**	**Monday**
Wednesday • Wepener occupied by Brabant • French and Tucker concentrate at Glen Siding	**28**	**Tuesday**
Thursday • Action at Karee Siding	**29**	**Wednesday**
Friday • Broadwood retires from Thaba'Nchu to Sannah's Post	**30**	**Thursday**
Saturday • Five VCs • Churchill leaves Natal and heads for Cape Town • Broadwood attacked by De Wet at Sannah's Post • Plumer in action at Ramathlabama	**31**	**Friday**

On Piet Joubert:

His eyes were both kindly and suspicious, his mouth both generous and selfish, and his beard was white when there was hardly a grey hair on his head. Although of hardened pioneering stock, he was sensitive, moody and as much a dreamer as he was an astute man of business.

Meintjies

On Louis Botha:

Like many men of his race Louis Botha had a bi-sexual temperament: his attachments were passionate and deep; his responses emotional and intuitive. Gracious to all women and deeply in love with his wife, Botha also needed the company of men at all times; he needed their talk, their warmth and affection as much as he needed air.

JOUBERT: 'PESSIMISTIC: TOO TIRED AT 68 TO MAKE A GREAT COMMANDER.' – LONGFORD

Christiaan De Wet

'Burly as he is, he is actively elusive to a degree that has often worsted us; yet he increased very considerably in weight as the war went on. He is not well educated but he is a sombre, steady fellow, endowed with much energy and with an amount of Boer doggedness that is tempered with common sense. He fought at Majuba Hill and, with Mr Gladstone's help, acquired so wholly wrong an impression of the British nature and the British flag, that he came to believe that the one was feeble and the other white. The common Englishman regards him with respect as a untiring fellow of the right sort, exceedingly wily, full of barbaric genius, whose sense helped to bring about peace.'

General Christiaan De Wet, who was born about 1852, springs from the ranks of the better educated Boers. His life has been spent in farming, which in his case meant growing 'mealies' (Indian corn) and forage for market. He amassed some fortune, but speculated rashly on the Johannesburg Stock Exchange and lost nearly all. He has taken part from time to time in minor native wars, but in no respect can he be said to have had anything approaching a military education. As a Free State burgher (he comes from the Harrismith district) he might have taken a prominent part in politics, but has preferred to remain comparatively aloof.

Christiaan Rudolf De Wet (1854-1922) emerged as the most brilliant military leader among the Free Staters and Steyn promptly raised him to Commander-in-Chief. De Wet was and looked like a farmer, athletic and stolid, cunning and inventive, but he was also a born leader, a superb tactician and had an instinctive military awareness.

JM

Having obtained leave from the S.A.H.L., Churchill applied to the *Morning Post* to get him accredited to Lord Roberts' Force in the Orange Free State. Whilst waiting for acceptance, and using the Mount Nelson Hotel as his temporary base, he visited Milner at Government House. Receiving no response to his application, however, he wrote to Ian Hamilton to make enquiries. The reply not encouraging, Churchill, anxious to join Roberts and Kitchener, had to accept that his 'free-flowing' pen had succeeded in offending both of them.

'THE BOERS WERE WORTHY AND CHIVALROUS FOES. THEY SHOWED NEITHER ARROGANCE NOR EXULTATION IN VICTORY AND TREATED THEIR WOUNDED ENEMIES WITH THE GREATEST CONSIDERATION.' – WBP

20.10.1899 Talana: Civilian without rank but military adviser to General Lucas Meyer
30.10.1899 General
30.3.1900 Commandant-General (acting), as time and circumstances did not permit voting. In Botha as his successor, Joubert had recognised that Botha's attributes would fulfil his own shortcomings. Botha's 'appointment' had been by special request granted by Kruger

Spioenkop:
Some dunderhead, perhaps, proposed that such guns should be taken by the army into the field – some fellow who had never read a civilized book on gunnery. But how many fools in history have led the world? Let us make ourselves wise men by adding another to the list.
JBA

Louis Botha (1862-1919): Soldier, statesman and first prime minister of the Union of South Africa (1910-1919): An opponent of both Kruger and of war with Britain, Louis Botha nevertheless joined his countrymen and eventually became Commander-in-Chief of the Boer Forces at Ladysmith (1900). He defeated the British at Colenso, Spioenkop and Vaalkrans.

When peace came back to the veld in 1902, Botha travelled to England (with Generals Koos de la Rey and Christiaan de Wet) to raise money for the reconstruction of his country and he was surprised to receive a hero's welcome there. He responded by labouring for conciliation between Boer and Briton in South Africa. That work bore fruit in 1910 when Louis Botha became the first Prime Minister of the Union of South Africa. Four years later he took his country into the Great War on England's side and cleared South West Africa of Germans. Louis Botha's enormous career ended at the age of 57; he left behind him the memory of a born soldier who yet was always filled with compassion for others' sufferings. General Jan Smuts was not exaggerating when he wrote of his friend that, 'He combined the strength of a man with the sensitiveness of a woman', and over Botha's grave Smuts burst out with, 'He was the cleanest, sweetest soul of all the land; of all my days'.

1900	APRIL	2000
Sunday • French moves to Waterval Drift in support of Broadwood	1	Saturday
Monday • ILH in Pietermaritzburg entrain for Elandslaagte to form part of the 2nd division under Clery • De Wet discovers DeWetsdorp deserted by the British who are marching to Reddersburg	2	Sunday

'BAD WATER CAN COST US MORE THAN ALL THE BULLETS OF THE ENEMY.'

The French connection: 'De Willeboer`

The Late General de Villebois-Mareuil

Sought out by Dr Leyds at the outbreak of hostilities, Count de Villebois-Mareuil, who retired from active service in the French Army in 1896, hastened to Africa, and set to work to elaborate a plan of campaign in Natal. He is said to have been responsible for the disposition of the Boers at Colenso and elsewhere on the Tugela, and to have been present and active in directing the repulse of Buller's attack. He was killed in action near Boshof, in the Orange Free State, where he and some seventy men were surrounded and killed or captured by Lord Methuen, April 5, 1900.

An outsider among the Boers: Colonel le Comte Georges de Villebois Mareuil in Liberte, Paris, 1900: The French Colonel: The only title used by the Boers who found his name unpronounceable, drew imprudent attention to technological backwardness of the Boers who were obliged to enlist foreign advisers, harped on the skills of Leon and Grunberg, two French gunnery experts from Creusot.

Relief! Along the banks of the Sundays River; 9 April 1900

'It has the merit of being true, but I am afraid that it won't sound half so funny as it looked. Yesterday I went down to the river to spy out the land, or rather water, with a view to washing me in the early morning.

While standing on the bank and contemplating the limped stream, (this is Poetical imagery, the actual colour of the water was Van Dyke Brown) I saw two Tommies approach. After a short interval one of them solemnly took off his boots and then plunged in with all his clothes on. He swam down the river for about 50 yards, and then swam back, came out, took a large cake of soap from his pal, and solemnly proceeded to soap himself all over, outside his clothes. Having finished all he could get at, he turned to his mate and said "ow's me back?" The other took his pipe out of his mouth, contemplated the others tunic and replied, "orrid." "Well soap it you chuchled 'eaded ijjit." So he of the pipe started and soaped his mate's back and having finished, pushed him into the river where he desported himself until he had washed all the soap out of his clothes, then he came ashore, and remarked that now he was alright, and went back to his camp. I thought it about the best scheme for saving time I had ever seen. It really doesn't look so funny, but I believe if someone like Kipling got hold of it and put in a real lot of swear words they would make something of it.'

AN INCIDENT REPORTED IN A LETTER TO HIS WIFE

Kitchener's resentment of Churchill dated from the 1897 Egyptian Campaign. Not having wanted Churchill in Egypt in the first place, he was outraged by criticisms of his campaign included in Churchill's *The River War*.

1900	APRIL	2000
Tuesday • Detachment of Royal Irish Rifles and Mounted Infantry surrounded near Reddersburg	**3**	Monday
Wednesday • Surrender of British detachment near Reddersburg • Clements arrives at Bloemfontein	**4**	Tuesday
Thursday • Villebois Mareuil killed in action near Boshof • Hunter at Rooidam	**5**	Wednesday
Friday • Owing to the losses and exhaustion of the cavalry horses at Karee Siding and Sannah's Post, Roberts is compelled to give up projected advance on Brandfort	**6**	Thursday
Saturday • Colonel Dalgety isolated at Jammersberg Drift, near Wepener	**7**	Friday
Sunday • De Wet so far very successful in his little raids *'Fortune rarely smiles on the leader underserving of her.'*	**8**	Saturday
Monday • Dalgety heavily attacked • General Gatacre superseded by General Chermside	**9**	Sunday

'Back-acher'

Lieutenant-General Sir William Forbes Gatacre K.C.B., D.S.O.

His dismissal

Born 1843. Entered the Army in 1862; was Instructor of Military Surveying at the Royal Military College, 1875-9; Deputy-Adjutant and Q.M.G. with the Hazara Expedition, 1888; served in Burma, 1889, Chitral, 1895; Soudan, 1898; and commanded the British Division at the battle of Khartoum; in command of South-Eastern District, 1898; appointed to command the 3rd Division in South Africa, with rank of Lieutenant-General, October, 1899. His two misfortunes at Stormberg and at Reddersburg were not calculated to inspire trust in the men he led, or the self-confidence essential to a commander. His personal bravery was beyond question, his zeal and love for his profession also undoubted. His failing was being almost without the sense of fatigue; he expected his men to be equally tireless. Soon after Reddersburg he was summoned to Bloemfontein by Lord Roberts and sent back to England, being replaced in his command of the Third Division by Major-General Chermside, who had previously had charge of the 14th Brigade in Tucker's Division.

Lady Sarah Wilson and her 'dug-out'

This adventurous lady, who represented the *Daily Mail* in the beleaguered town, is the wife of Captain Gordon C. Wilson, and daughter of the seventh Duke of Marlborough. At the beginning of the siege she left Mafeking and rode to Setlagoli, and afterwards went to Mosuti and Vryburg, arranging for the running of despatches to and from Mafeking. She endeavoured to get back into the town, but the Boers refused to give her up except in exchange for Viljoen, a notorious horse-thief. It was one of her silk dresses, 'commandeered' by General Cronje, which graced the arm of Mrs Cronje as she stepped into the train for Capetown on the way to St Helena.

Lord Roberts owed his appointment as Commander-in-Chief: India, to Randolph Churchill. As a friend of the family, his own Freddy only two years older than Winston, Roberts' indulgence of the young correspondent was tried to the limit by an outspoken despatch in the *Morning Post* in February; some pointed remarks about the foolish formality of a sermon preached by an army chaplain shortly before the final breakthrough in Natal. The devout Lord Roberts, feeling that his chaplains had been slighted, was aggrieved, and only relented after the all-out efforts of mutual friends.

1900	APRIL	2000
Tuesday • Determined attack on Wepener position repulsed • Boers shell Elandslaagte camp	**10**	Monday
Wednesday • Mafeking heavily bombarded • Reddersburg re-occupied by Chermside • General Gatacre ordered home	**11**	Tuesday
Thursday • Wepener, a little town on the Basuto border, named after Commandant Wepener who took part in the 1865-8 Basuto War	**12**	Wednesday
Friday • Wepener under siege – one of the noteworthy incidents of the War	**13**	Thursday
Saturday • Sir George White arrives at Southhampton	**14**	Friday
Sunday • Hart, Brabant and Chermside start for the relief of Dalgety • Boer delegates arrive at The Hague	**15**	Saturday
Monday • Rouxville occupied by Major Cumming • Continuous rain – half filling the trenches with water	**16**	Sunday

Besieged Towns		Relieved	Total days
Kimberley:	16 October 1899	15 February 1900	123
Mafeking:	16 October 1899	17 April 1900	184
Ladysmith:	02 November 1899	28 February 1900	118

Lieutenant-General Reginald Pole-Carew, C.B., J.P.

Born in Cornwall in 1849 and educated at Eton and Christ Church, Oxford. Entered the Coldstream Guards, 1869; Private Secretary to Sir Hercules Robinson, Governor of New South Wales, 1876-7; A.D.C. to Lord Lytton, Viceroy of India, 1878-9; to Sir Frederick (now Lord) Roberts in the Afghan War, 1879-80; and to H.R.H. the Duke of Connaught in Egypt, 1882; Lieutenant-Colonel, 1883; Military Secretary to Sir F. Roberts in India, 1884-90; served in the Burmese Expedition of 1886-7; Colonel 1888; commanded the 2nd Battalion Coldstream Guards, 1895-9; Brigadier-General in command of a 2nd class District in India, 1899; Major-General, 1899; commands the Eleventh Division in South Africa with local rank of Lieutenant-General.

World debut of the field telephone in war:
A control post or 'conning tower' for the Naval guns was established and connected by field telephone to the batteries, and Sir George White's HQs were also linked into the network. A similar system was used in Kimberley and Mafeking.

Harry Beet: Corporal (later Captain): 1st Battalion: The Derbyshire Regiment:
Gazetted 12 Feb 1901
22 April 1900: Wakkerstroom: An infantry company and two squadrons of the Imperial Yeomanry had to retire from a farm under a ridge held by the Boers. A corporal was lying on the ground wounded and Corporal Beet, seeing him, remained behind and put him under cover, bound up his wounds and, by firing, prevented the enemy from coming down to the farm until dark when a medical officer came to the wounded man's assistance. Corporal Beet was exposed to very heavy fire during the whole afternoon.

1900	APRIL	2000
Tuesday • Formation of Mafeking relief column under Colonel Mahon ordered	**17**	Monday
Wednesday • Rundle and Chermside advance on Dewetsdorp	**18**	Tuesday
Thursday • Scouts confined to trenches day and night – nothing but cold food and water for supper every evening	**19**	Wednesday
Friday • Rundle engaged near Dewetsdorp • Boer positions attacked	**20**	Thursday
Saturday • Messages from Lord Roberts kept coming through to say that help was at hand • Ammunition getting very low	**21**	Friday
Sunday • One VC • Pole-Carew: 11th Division attacks Lemmer at Leeuw Kop	**22**	Saturday
Monday • 10th Division arrives at Kimberley from Natal • Ian Hamilton re-captures the Waterworks at Sannah's Post	**23**	Sunday

Sir George White

Defender of Ladysmith:

'Amidst the general praise there must be some blame. There was one old lady who behaved most shabbily. I had protected her all the time of the siege, but no sooner was she under the protection of General Buller than she gave me a very hot time, never allowing my temperature to go up under 103. I refer to Lady … Smith!'

CAPTAIN LAMBTON'S REFERENCE TO SIR GEORGE WHITE DURING A CELEBRATION BANQUET IN THE TOWN HALL, PORTSMOUTH, 24 APRIL 1900:

**In saving Ladysmith he saved Natal,
In saving Natal he saved South Africa,
And, in saving South Africa he saved the Empire.**

That Dormant Commission

Signed by Queen Victoria on December 2nd, it states:

'We, reposing especial trust and confidence in your loyalty, courage and good conduct, do by these presents constitute and appoint you to have the local rank of General in Our Land Forces on the decease or incapacity from any cause to exercise command, of General the Right Honourable Sir Redvers Henry Buller, GCB, KCMG, VC. And we do hereby give and grant you full power and authority to assume command as General Officer Commanding-in-Chief Our Land Forces in South Africa and to take your rank accordingly.'

Warren had sailed to Cape town without any knowledge that he was to be appointed Buller's Second-in-Command, and still less with any suspicion that he was to receive a Dormant Commission as Commander-in-Chief, but on his arrival he found a telegram from Wolseley informing him of these facts, and later received the following letter dated December 6th:

You will have found a telegram awaiting your arrival at Cape Town informing you that in the event of any accident overtaking Sir Redvers Buller you are to take supreme command in South Africa. A Dormant Commission goes out to you by this post.

I look to Sir Redvers Buller and to you to put an end to this folly.

'That dug-up Policeman' (BULLER OF WARREN)

Punch to the Peelers: Caricature of Sir Charles Warren, controversial Chief Commissioner of Police. He resigned at the close of the Ripper murders, and few shed any tears.

1887: The Whitechapel murders came at a time when popular discontent with the Metropolitan Police was at a peak. A recently appointed Chief Commissioner, Sir Charles Warren, headed the force. Sir Charles was an army man, first and foremost. He filled five new senior police posts with army officers and introduced military discipline into a civilian force.

When the Ripper murders erupted and the killer remained free, hostile newspapers sniped away at Warren unmercifully. They branded him as inept, inflexible, and damaging to police morale.

'GHASTLY MURDER! REVOLTING AND MYSTERIOUS MURDER! EAST END HORRORS! DREADFUL MUTILATION OF A WOMAN!'
… SOME OF THE GARISH NEWSPAPER HEADLINES THAT PETRIFIED ALL ENGLAND IN 1888.

1900	APRIL	2000
Tuesday • Boers again attack Dalgety, but are repulsed • Boer position at Warrenton bombarded • Explosion at the Begbie factory in Johannesburg	**24**	Monday
Wednesday • Dalgety relieved • Boers retire from Wepener and Dewetsdorp • Hamilton and Grobler engaged at Israel's Poort	**25**	Tuesday
Thursday • Sir Charles Warren appointed Governor of Griqualand West	**26**	Wednesday
Friday • French and Ian Hamilton at Thaba'Nchu	**27**	Thursday
Saturday • Fighting near Thaba'Nchu mountain	**28**	Friday
Sunday *'Mafeking food situation serious. Locusts provided yet another source - especially for the Barolong in the Stadt.'* – SOL PLAATJE	**29**	Saturday
Monday • Ian Hamilton attacks Boers at Houtnek • Tucker engaged at KrantzKraal • British subjects expelled from the Transvaal • Queen Victoria receives White at Windsor	**30**	Sunday

The Terrible

A terrible lot you terribles
And a terrible name you bear
And a terrible welcome we'll give to you
When we think of your actions there.

You went to the front at a terrible pace
You took a terrible four inch gun
Spread terrible dead around the place
'Til the Boers were forced to run

It wasn't a superior force they feared
but the terrible terrible fire
If what I relate isn't the Gospel Truth
I'm a terrible handy liar.

The whole way up the line there was to be an exasperating monotony in the proceedings of both sides, which makes this portion of the campaign one of the least interesting in military history.

LA

One of the 4.7″ naval guns shelling Grobler's Kloof

'SMELLY INSTINCTS: WHEN UNCERTAIN OF THE ROAD IN THE DARK I MADE FOR WHAT LOOKED LIKE, OR RATHER SMELT LIKE, DEAD HORSE OR BULLOCKS – FINE LANDMARKS, AN EXCELLENT GUIDE ON THE VELDT WHEN ONE IS IN DIFFICULTY.' – WK-LD

1900	MAY	2000
Tuesday • Boers driven from Houtnek by Ian Hamilton • Gen Hart occupies Smithfield	**1**	Monday
Wednesday • Queen Victoria receives *Powerful's* Naval Brigade at Windsor	**2**	Tuesday
Thursday • Lord Roberts occupies Brandfort • Siege guns landed at Cape Town	**3**	Wednesday
Friday • Mafeking relief column under Colonel Mahon starts from Barkly West • Hunter crosses Vaal at Windsorton • Warren, appointed Military Governor of Griqualand West, arrives at Orange River • Ian Hamilton drives the Boers off the Baviaansberg	**4**	Thursday
Saturday • Hunter successfully engages Boers at Rooidam • Action at Vet River • Hamilton occupies Winburg • White and Lambton guests of honour at Royal Academy banquet	**5**	Friday
Sunday • Vet River passed and Smaldeel occupied	**6**	Saturday
Monday • Hunter joins Paget at Fourteen Streams • Transvaal Volksraad meets for the last time	**7**	Sunday

Buller:

Colonel R.B. Hawley, a first-rate commanding officer, and an enormous advantage to a young man serving under him, realized best by those not equally fortunate:

'Every single thing connected with the food, comfort, and training of a regiment was brought by Hawley to its highest pitch of perfection ... among his many distinguished pupils his most brilliant was Redvers Buller.'

Although there is a considerable undercurrent of hostile and venomous criticism, upon the whole I have gained considerably by what has passed since I have been in South Africa.

WSCH TO HIS MOTHER: 1 MAY 1900

1900	MAY 2000
Tuesday • Buller commences his advance from Ladysmith • Carrington's advance troops reach Bulawayo • Brabant reaches Thaba'Nchu	**8** Monday
Wednesday • Mahon reaches Vryburg • Capture of Welgelegen	**9** Tuesday
Thursday • Lord Roberts forces passage of the Zand River • Occupation of Ventersburg	**10** Wednesday
Friday • Buller at Waschbank River • Mr Chamberlain at Birmingham announces Government's intention to annex Republics	**11** Thursday
Saturday • Kroonstad occupied • Attack on Mafeking repulsed and Commandant Eloff captured	**12** Friday
Sunday • Mahon beats off Liebenberg's attack at Koedoesrand • General Buller advances towards Biggarsberg	**13** Saturday
Monday • Buller drives the Boers from the Biggarsberg and occupies Dundee	**14** Sunday

1893: Buller: He was pressed to accept, but declined, the post of Commander-in-Chief in India. During his stay in China two misadventures attended the ensign. He was so nearly drowned that he was thought dead when pulled out of the water; and a horse kicked out his front teeth, thus making his speech a little indistinct for the rest of his life.

An ode in 'B'

Buller brought his brave British Brigades
To battle with Botha's Boer's,
And he backed of his biscuits and baccy and beer
He was bringing to Ladysmith doors.

Bully for Buller! Well blown out
With beer and brandy and cheek,
He bounced in his beautiful way
He'd be beseiged in a week

But the Boers have banished his bright idea
And his brows are bent and black;
For the bullets have bizzed and the bombshells burst,
But Buller is beaten back.

The bubble is burst and bellies bawl
For bread to make them fuller
But the belly is balked by the man who talked
Poor belly, poor bungling Buller.

The result of an officer of the I L H who could not resist the temptation to try his hand at composition as the Relieving Force advanced or retired, the Ladysmith garrison filled with either keen hope or deep despondancy. To utter the name 'Buller' meant paying some sort of penalty.

GENERAL SIR GEORGE WHITE ON THE IMPERIAL LIGHT HORSE

The Imperial Light Horse rendered magnificent services throughout that never-to-to-be-forgotten period. Speaking with the experience of fifty years of soldiering my testimony is that I have never commanded a more gallant or more serviceable force than that of the Imperial Light Horse. Of such stuff are the ranks of the maligned Uitlanders of the Transvaal, from the towns and villages of the Cape or Natal, from Canada, Australia, Birman, Ceylon or from the towns and cities of the motherland herself.

VC

John Mackay: Lance-Corporal (later Lieutenant-Colonel) 1st Battalion: The Gordon Highlanders: *Gazetted 10 Aug 1900*

20 May 1900: During the action on Crow's Nest Hill, Johannesburg, Corporal Mackay repeatedly rushed forward under withering fire at short range to attend to wounded comrades and dress their wounds. He was himself without shelter and on one occasion he carried a wounded man from the open, under fire, to the shelter of a boulder.

Ian Hamilton: Tall, thin Colonel. Churchill met him on board ship from India. Hamilton was one of the few British Generals favourably disposed to the controversial *Morning Post* correspondent. No longer the hero who had escaped from the Boers, Churchill was regarded as an interfering newspaperman not content with fighting and reporting, but now tempted to try his hand at peace-making.

'THE TIDE, HAVING TURNED FOR THE BRITISH; THE MILITARY CAMPAIGN APPARENTLY DRAWING TO A CLOSE; POLITICAL CONSIDERATIONS NOW LOOMED LARGER THAN ENEMY OPPOSITION.' – BR

1900	MAY	2000
Tuesday • Natal Army re-occupies Dundee • Hunter enters Transvaal on Western border • Lord Methuen advances from Boshoff • Mahon joins Plumer • Glencoe occupied	**15**	Monday
Wednesday • Hunter occupies Christiana • Mahon and Plumer defeat Boers under De la Rey at Israel's Farm	**16**	Tuesday
Thursday • Buller enters Newcastle • Churchill, officially a non-combatant, re-joins Hamilton • Relief of Mafeking • Ladybrand and Clocolan occupied by Colonial Division	**17**	Wednesday
Friday • Buller occupies Newcastle • Methuen enters Hoopstad • Ian Hamilton occupies Lindley	**18**	Thursday
Saturday • Dundonald advances to Laing's Nek *'The Army lay under the loom of Majuba which had cast its sinister shadow for so long over South African politics.'*	**19**	Friday
Sunday • One VC • Bethune's Mounted Infantry surprised at Scheeper's Nek near Vryheid	**20**	Saturday
Monday • Warren captures Douglas	**21**	Sunday

'AS A BUDDING POLITICIAN, CHURCHILL HAD THOUGHT IT OPPORTUNE TO VOICE HIS OPINIONS ABOUT ANY FUTURE SETTLEMENT OF HOSTILITIES.' – BR

The Queen has throughout the war shown the greatest solicitude for the wounded. On March 22, 1900, Her Majesty paid a visit to the Herbert Hospital at Woolwich, and personally handed gifts of flowers to over a hundred wounded men, in each case accompanying the gift with a few words of sympathy, which often had reference to the services of the particular man she addressed. The patients included survivors from Colenso and Spioenkop. The Irish soldiers, whose gallantry had been specially noteworthy, were favoured with special notice.

The crowning of a great career

Her Majesty, Queen Victoria, bestowing an Earldom on Lord Roberts at Osborne, January 2, 1901. A pathetic interest attaches to this act, which was the last of importance carried out by Her Majesty in person. It is known that Lord Roberts was greatly moved by this interview, and it is safe to assume that the Queen herself realised that it marked the end of her reign.

Not all the generals welcomed Churchill's presence with their columns. Word had got around that the cocksure subaltern-cum-war-correspondent was frowned upon by Roberts, and that he could be very critical, commanded a large audience and was not to be trusted.

1900	MAY	2000
Tuesday • Main army advances from Kroonstad • Ian Hamilton at Heilbron • Colvile leaves Winburg	**22**	Monday
Wednesday • Hunter reaches Vryburg • Rhenoster position turned	**23**	Tuesday
Thursday • Queen Victoria's last birthday • Annexation of the OFS proclaimed and renamed Orange River Colony • French crosses the Vaal near Parys • Methuen marches to Bothaville • Colvile leaves Ventersburg for Heilbron	**24**	Wednesday
Friday • Rundle occupies Senekal • Spragge and Irish Yeomanry leave Krooonstad for Lindley	**25**	Thursday
Saturday • Baden-Powell enters Zeerust • Colvile reaches Lindley	**26**	Friday
Sunday • Main army crosses Vaal at Vereeniging • Boers retire to Klip River Station	**27**	Saturday
Monday • French crosses the Klip River and attacks Boers near Van Wyk's Rust • Colvile in action at Rooipoort • Colonel Adye defeats Prieska rebels at Kheirs • Methuen arrives at Kroonstad	**28**	Sunday

'One of the most photographed men in the world, the one to feature in endless cartoons.'

Stephanus Johannes Paulus Kruger

'He typified the Boer character both in its brighter and darker aspects and was no doubt the greatest man – both morally and intellectually – whom the Boer race so far produced. In his iron will tenacity, his "never say die" attitude towards fate, his mystic faith in another world, he represented what is best in all of us.'

SMUTS TO HOBHOUSE ON KRUGER'S DEATH DEC. 1904

KROOGER

There was an old man of Pretoria
Whose conduct got gorier and gorier,
When a piece of shell
Sent him screaming to …
Well he has vacated his place to Victoria.

There are some faces that have nothing to do with beauty or ugliness – faces beyond time and place, faces that never blur, never remind you of anybody else and always involve a slight shock of recognition.

JM

Off with his thumb!

Mr Kruger had the thumb of his left hand shattered in a gun accident. He amputated it himself with a knife when gangrene set in.

'He is the central figure of South African history – but to extract the man as a personality from a veritable bog of hostility and sentiment, prejudice and deification.'

Age was to bring its ravages, particularly an affliction of the eyes; but it is said that even well beyond middle age women were fascinated by Kruger's virility, even that they threw themselves at him – rather hopelessly, for he was no philanderer.

The Bloemfontein Conference: 31 May – 5th June 1899

When Milner demanded prompt and wholesale reform of the franchise, Kruger cried: 'It is our country you want!'

The conference ending in stalemate, the Boers amassed arms in the Transvaal; British troopships were despatched to the Cape.

'THE KEY TO THE PHENOMENON OF KRUGER WAS HIS IMPLICIT BELIEF THAT HE WAS *CALLED* BY GOD.' – JM

1900	MAY	2000
Tuesday • Main army at Germiston • Battle of Doornkop • Ian Hamilton occupies Florida • Rundle heavily engaged at Biddulphsberg • Irish Yeomanry in difficulties at Lindley • Colvile arrives at Heilbron	**29**	Monday
Wednesday • Methuen leaves Kroonstad to relieve Irish Yeomanry • Kruger leaves Pretoria for Machadodorp • Boers attack Warren at Faber's Put	**30**	Tuesday
Thursday • Capture of Johannesburg • Surrender of 500 Irish Yeomanry near Lindley	**31**	Wednesday

Once more o'er Transvaal hills and plains
Our flag's four colours blow;
And woe to the ungodly hand
That tries to bring it low!
Then, flag of freedom, wave aloft,
The air is bright and clear,
Our enemies are put to flight,
More joyous days are near.

Translation of the Transvaal National Hymn

BLACK AND WHITE
APRIL 1900

Louis Napoleon

'But in 1879, when he was but 23, he took a step that doomed them all. Too bold and too reckless, too exuberant and something of a show-off, he even offended the British Army's greatest exhibitionist warrior, Redvers Buller.'

Discovery of the body ... 'I was riding by the side of Forbes (Daily News), when, a short distance on our left, we saw one of the troop holding up his rifle and calling out loud. Forbes immediately said, "There it is, Prior. Come on, ride for it!" and a magnificent rider he was.

I followed hard on his heels, and was the fourth man to arrive on the spot. (General Evelyn Wood and Colonel Buller were there first). There I saw the Prince Imperial lying on his back, stark-naked, with a thin gold chain round his neck, to which was attached a locket containing the portrait of his father, the late Emperor Napoleon the Third. The Zulus had stripped him, and taken away every particle of clothing, but, looking upon this gold chain and locket as a fetish, had respected it, and left it still round his neck.

Melton Prior

'Louis, however, became a nagging worry to his father. In his studies he was bored and listless. His standard of scholarship was low. Faced with a mathematical problem he would stare into space in bewilderment, disturbing his tutor Filon with the confession that he simply did not know what it was all about. But as soon as Louis escaped Filon and his school books into the society of other people, he seemed to become another person. There had evolved in the youth an all-conquering charm. He was smaller than average height. He had a pleasant face but no startling good looks. But his nature, even at its most mischievous, possessed a beauty and attractiveness that drew love and respect from his friends and acquaintances, from Queen Victoria etc. It was a mutual friend of Napoleon and the Prince of Wales who suggested that Louis should apply to become a gentleman cadet at the Royal Military Academy at Woolwich, then the great centre of training in engineering and gunnery. When the academy – *The Shop* – was mentioned, he reacted with enthusiasm. His listlessness, and what Filon thought was lack of understanding, vanished. He worked with keen concentration for the entrance examination to *The Shop* – and he passed. As a cadet at the academy the prince was an unqualified success. At drill, at examinations, parades and inspections he shone. The Governor of the Academy marvelled that a youth with such a strange and un-British background should become so easily and painlessly integrated with his British cadets. Louis differed from the others only in that he did not play games (sport).'

JOHN WALTERS: ALDERSHOT REVIEW P89 PARALLEL TO WINSTON CHURCHILL

VC

Frank Kirby: Corporal (later Lieutenant-Colonel): Corps of Royal Engineers:
Gazetted 5 Oct 1900

2 June 1900: Near Delagoa Bay Railway: During the retirement of a small party being hotly pressed by superior numbers of the enemy, Corporal Kirby turned and rode back to help a man whose horse had been shot. Although by the time he reached the man they were under heavy fire at close range, Corporal Kirby managed to get the man up behind him and took him clear of the firing. This was the third occasion on which Corporal Kirby has shown gallantry in the face of the enemy.

'HOW IS IT, THEN, THAT YOU ARE ALIVE?'

– BULLER TO OFFICER WHO HAD GONE OUT WITH THE ILL-FATED PRINCE IMPERIAL WHEN HE RETURNED TO REPORT HIS DEATH.

'THE RAILWAYS IN THE FREE STATE: IN THE MINDS OF RURAL PEOPLE, THE RAILWAYS REPRESENTED THE EVILS OF FOREIGN CIVILIZATION, AND THEY WANTED NO PART OF THEM.'

History repeating itself?:

The language question

Although Dutch was the official language of the Free State, English was still spoken extensively, and Steyn was worried that, because of the inflow of immigrants, and that so many of the officials were English, the people might forget to cherish their own tongue. He warned them that the language was in fact the people, and that if they allowed it to be dissipated, they in turn would be lost.

Learn other languages by all means, but keep your own pure and loved above all others.

Steyn

1900	JUNE	2000
Friday • Union Jack hoisted at Pretoria • Methuen re-occupies Lindley • Lord Roberts issues a third proclamation to Boers • Boer Council at Pretoria resolves to continue guerrilla warfare	**1**	Thursday
Saturday • One VC • Buller and Christiaan Botha meet at Laing's Nek • Kosi Bay expedition abandoned	**2**	Friday
Sunday *'Pretoria, a place which by-and-by should have its name most properly changed in honour of Victoria.'*	**3**	Saturday
Monday • De Wet captures Heilbron convoy at Zwavelkranz • French occupies Commando and Zilikat's Nek • Warren enters Campbell	**4**	Sunday

'BULLER RULED HIS MEN WITH A ROD OF IRON, YET WHILE THEY FEARED HIM THEY HAD A DOG-LIKE LOVE FOR HIM.'

The capture of Pretoria, with its consequent disruption of Boer communications with the outside world and loss to them of their entire armament industry, made ultimate victory inevitable. If it did not result in the immediate end of hostilities as the Commander-in-Chief hoped, this was largely due to the impossibility of bringing the enemy to pitched battle.

Like the waves of the sea before a man-of-war they parted before the advance of the great army, only to gather round it again when it passed on.

The 'Lion of the West': **De la Rey**

.... But the pens were dropped, and the Mauser and the Lee-Metford once more took up the debate.

From the moral and political standpoint, it had always been Roberts' hope that the conquest of both capitals would lead to a desire for peace and it was for this very reason that he had hitherto treated the enemy with such clemency.

5 June: Botha calls a meeting of the Transvaal leaders a short distance from the city. Held in an aura of deepest gloom, surrender is freely talked of ...

8 June: Mrs Botha visits Roberts as her husband's emissary, stating for certain that both he and De la Rey are anxious to surrender and requests an interview for them ...

At this critical moment, when the issue of peace hung in the very balance, news was brought of De Wet's great successes on the line of communication and immediately the Boer attitude hardened and the chance was lost ... for two years to come.

'THE MODEL SCHOOL, PRETORIA, NOW A HOSPITAL FOR BRITISH SOLDIERS, RECENTLY THE PRISON OF OUR OFFICERS.'

1900	**JUNE**	**2000**
Tuesday • Capture of Pretoria • Botha refuses terms of surrender offered by Buller • Boer leaders meet near Eerstefabrieken *'The first British flag was hoisted over Pretoria – time 8:47.'*	**5**	Monday
Wednesday • British prisoners released at Waterval • Cape Ministers advocate withdrawal of martial law	**6**	Tuesday
Thursday • Hunter enters Ventersdorp • Griquatown occupied by Warren • 4th Derbyshires overwhelmed by De Wet at Renoster River (Rodewal) • Lord Roberts proposes a meeting with Louis Botha	**7**	Wednesday
Friday • Capture of Botha's Pass by Buller's forces	**8**	Thursday
Saturday • Klerksdorp surrendered to Hunter	**9**	Friday
Sunday • Churchill prepares to leave *'South Africa had served its purpose and served it well.'*	**10**	Saturday
Monday • Battle of Alleman's Nek • Lord Roberts engages Boers at Diamond Hill • Mahon captures Potchefstroom	**11**	Sunday

The little bronze cross

The biggest award eludes both Churchill and Hamilton

During the South African War, Winston gave the embattled hosts at Diamond Hill an exhibition of conspicuous gallantry (the phrase often used in recommendations for the VC) for which he has never received full credit. Here is the story:

'My column, including Broadwood's Cavalry and a lot of guns, lay opposite and below a grassy mountain, bare of rocks or trees, not unlike our own South Downs where they meet the sea. The crest line was held by the Boer left. The key to the battlefield lay on the summit but nobody knew it until Winston, who had been attached to my Column by the High Command, somehow managed to give me the slip and to climb this mountain, most of it being dead ground to the Boers lining the crestline as they had to keep their heads down owing to our heavy gun-fire. He climbed this mountain as our Scouts were trained to climb on the Indian Frontier and ensconced himself in a niche not much more than a pistol shot directly below the Boer Commandos – no mean feat of arms in broad daylight and showing a fine trust in the accuracy of our own guns. Had even half a dozen of the Burghers run twenty yards over the brow they could have knocked him off his perch with a volley of stones. Thus it was that from his lofty perch Winston had the nerve to signal me, if I remember right, with his handkerchief on a stick, that if I could only manage to gallop up at the head of my Mounted Infantry we ought to be able to rush the summit. At that moment another message was handed in from Sir John French saying that our extreme left was falling back. A strong counter-stroke seemed therefore as if it might come in the nick of time. Lord Airlie's charge (and death) at the head of his Lancers had for the moment completely cleared the face of the mountain – there was nothing moving but a field ambulance – so I called up my men and jumped on to my little black waler. Before I had got my right foot into the stirrup (luckily) a blow like a punch from the fist of a giant struck my right shoulder and I was flung out of the saddle. A shrapnel bullet had struck me, but the range being extreme had only decorated my back with a big black and blue bruise, nothing more, no blood, no wound pension, no nothing, so on we galloped. Pole Carew and the Guards followed suit and we were right in among the Boers firing from horseback, a most glorious scrimmage, before they knew where they were; but they were in the soup all right and lo and behold! the left flank of the Boers was turned. Looks quite simple, doesn't it – on paper? Louis Botha has himself told us in his memoirs how he had been on the point of delivering a crushing blow at French and his Cavalry on our extreme left which would have sent him (so Botha was persuaded) scampering back to Pretoria when, his own left having turned, he had to forgo his coup and fall back with the whole of his force.

The capture of Diamond Hill meant the winning of the battle, ending as it did in a general retirement by the Boers; also it meant the turning point of the war. The capture of Pretoria had not been the true turning point but rather this battle of Diamond Hill which proved that, humanly speaking, Pretoria would not be retaken.

Persistent efforts were made by me to get some mention made or notice taken of Winston's initiative and daring and of how he had grasped the whole lay-out of the battlefield; but he had two big dislikes against him, – those of Bobs and K. And he had only been a Press Correspondent – they declared – so nothing happened. As it was under me at Gudda Kulai that he had enjoyed a brief but very strenuous course of study in the art of using ground to the best advantage either for attack or defence, this made me furious with impotent rage and I would like the number of penmen who are making good copy out of Winston every day to bear this fact more constantly in mind: that he had his full share of bad luck as well as of good before he reached his present high perch on the political Diamond Hill, where now everyone shouts bravo! each time he opens his mouth.'

I.H.

If one is familiar with the lay-out and details of the battle of Spioenkop, it is amazing to realise what natural grasp Churchill had, to the extent that as a young twenty-five year old correspondent-cum-2nd Lieutenant in the South African Light Horse, he dared to bother Sir Charles Warren until he listened to him. At Spioenkop he had also disobeyed strict orders to stay off the battlefield. He not only climbed up the hill to sum up the situation for himself, but in fact took a written instruction from Warren to Thorneycroft on the summit.

M.R.

Ian Hamilton and the elusive VC

27 February 1881

'As to my personal experiences, I had shave after shave – close shaves too – with Death on this Hill of Destiny: Majuba,'... after which Sir Evelyn Wood had recommended Hamilton for the VC. Denied the coveted award on this occasion because Wood had not personally seen the action, along with the excuse that he was young enough to have a second chance, he was again denied the award for valour at Elandslaagte as the 'act for which he was recommended was performed when he was commanding a Brigade, ie. in the position of a General Officer. The Victoria Cross has never been conferred upon an Officer so high in rank.'

'I HAVE A GOOD BELIEF THAT I AM TO BE OF SOME USE AND THEREFORE TO BE SPARED.' – WSCH

1900	JUNE	2000
Tuesday • Battle of Diamond Hill • Buller occupies Volksrust • Boers evacuate Laing's Nek • Carrington's 1st Brigade arrives at Bulawayo	**12**	Monday
Wednesday • Resignation of the Schreiner Ministry • Lyttelton occupies Wakkerstroom	**13**	Tuesday
Thursday • Boer attack on Zand River post repulsed by Colonel Capper • Rustenburg occupied by Baden-Powell	**14**	Wednesday
Friday • Column left Pretoria to meet Baden-Powell and to repair telegraph between Pretoria and Rustenberg	**15**	Thursday
Saturday • Hunter leaves Potchefstroom to command Hamilton's Column at Heidelberg	**16**	Friday
Sunday • Streinaecker's Horse blow up a bridge near Kaap Muiden	**17**	Saturday
Monday • Baden-Powell arrives at Pretoria • Hunter occupies Krugersdorp	**18**	Sunday

Field-Marshal Lord Roberts

of Kandahar and Waterford, V.C., K.P., G.C.B., G.C.S.I., G.C.I.E.

This portrait, perhaps better than any other of the many which exist, brings before one the true character of this great soldier. There is no fencing with the steady, penetrating, and yet not unkindly gaze of the eyes. The whole face speaks of that perfectly-balanced combination of justice and mercy, vigour and refinement, inflexibility and consummate tact, which have made Lord Roberts equally loved and feared. 'His army,' says Mr Julian Ralph with absolute truthfulness, 'will do anything for him; march longer, starve harder, go without tents, blankets, and run more days and weeks, and die in greater numbers for him than for any other man alive.'

I look to Sir Redvers Buller and to you to put an end to this folly. Our men and Regimental Officers have done splendidly. Our Generals so far have been our weak point. I am very anxious to push on good Colonels, so please let me know the names of those whom you think promising. If you have time please let me hear from you now and then, and write your own views freely on everything. May God bless you is the devout prayer of yours very sincerely, Wolseley.

The appointment of Lord Roberts as a result of Buller's severe reverse at Colenso meant the cancellation of Buller's appointment as Commander-in-Chief for South Africa, though he retained his post as Commander-in-Chief of the Natal Field Force; while Warren's Dormant Commission as Commander-in-Chief for South Africa was likewise invalidated by the changes in supreme command, and he remained with Buller as his Second-in-Command in the Natal Field Force.

Roberts: 'Whom neither ease nor honours moved
An hair's breadth from his aim.' – KIPLING

Roberts: 'Not a successful automaton but a human being carrying a great load of sorrow'.

Buller: 'But just before joining his regiment he very nearly put an end to everything. He was up in a tree in the woods at Downes, lopping, when he cut his right leg so severely that the Devonshire doctor declared it must be amputated or else he would die. Redvers Buller stoutly replied that he would rather die with two legs than live with one, and he was eventually cured.'

It is one of the principal criticisms of Roberts' conduct of the war, and probably the best founded, that he did not either enforce his views on Buller or else send him home and replace him by a more enterprising commander. His principal reason for retaining him and conceding so much to 'keep him sweet' was that no matter how slow and disheartened Buller might be, he was at least fairly safe and there was no one of sufficient seniority proven better to put in his place. His subsidiary motives may perhaps have been over-chivalrous but they were only pointers to the same solution. He dreaded the scandal to the Army were he forced to send him home, much as he would have liked to do so; and he was reluctant to treat the man he had superseded like any other subordinate commander. Finally, though this he was only to mention once and that many years later, in his heart Roberts always attributed his son's death to Buller's culpably mishandled attack on Colenso, and this conclusion made him all the more anxious not to risk being personally unfair to the man. So Buller retained his command.

... I suppose I ought to have felt proud and happy this morning (he wrote to his wife) when Kitchener congratulated me on being across the Vaal, but the rent in my heart seems to stifle all feelings of joy and pleasure. I could not help thinking how very different it would have been if our dear boy had been with me. Honours, rewards and congratulations have no value to me. So very different to what they were when I used to think of the son who would bear my name. But I must not write like this. God for some wise purposes has taken our dear Freddy from us and we must try and say 'thy will be done! ...

1900	JUNE	2000
Tuesday • De Wet attacks Methuen with a convoy near Heilbron	**19**	Monday
Wednesday • Extinction of rebellion in Cape Colony • De Villiers surrenders	**20**	Tuesday
Thursday • His decision to leave South Africa was a political one • Only by returning now could he hope to be in a position to contest the Oldham Seat	**21**	Wednesday
Friday • Buller's troops enter Standerton • Railway cut at Serfontein America Siding • Attack by Olivier on Katbosch beaten off • Dundonald occupies Standerton	**22**	Thursday
Saturday • Ian Hamilton captures Heidelberg • Clements attacked between Winburg and Senekal	**23**	Friday
Sunday • Clements defeats the Boers at Winburg	**24**	Saturday
Monday • Grenfell surprised at Leliefontein, near Senekal	**25**	Sunday

VC

Last VC winner to be decorated by Queen Victoria

Charles Ward: Private (later Sergeant-Major) 2nd Battalion: The King's Own Yorkshire Light Infantry: *Gazetted 28 September 1900*

26 June 1900: Lindley: A piquet of the regiment was surrounded on three sides by about 500 Boers and the majority of them were either killed or wounded. Private Ward volunteered to take a message asking for reinforcements to the signalling post about 150 yards away. He was eventually allowed to go, although it seemed certain that he would be shot, and he managed to get across through a storm of bullets. Having delivered his message, he returned to his commanding officer across the fire-swept ground, and was severely wounded, but his gallant action saved the post from capture.

Major-General Coke

John Talbot Coke was educated at Harrow; entered the Army as 2nd Lieutenant in the 21st Foot in 1859, and was transferred to the 25th Foot (afterwards named the King's Own Scottish Borderers) in 1860; Captain 1866; Major, 1879; Lieutenant-Colonel 1885; Colonel, 1889; was put on half-pay, 1898. He served with the Suakin Field Force in 1888 during the Investment of Suakin; was present in the engagement of Gemaizah; served in the operations on the Sudan frontier in 1889; was appointed senior officer at Mauritius in 1898, with local rank of Major-General; and left there to command the 10th Brigade of the South African Field Force, 1899.

Unthinking machines

'Hampered by tradition and the lack of effective training, the British soldier was, in the words of Lord Wolseley "the worst paid labourer in England". Often illiterate and unskilled, his military knowledge was confined to three weeks of field training and route marches during the year. For the rest he was parading and polishing equipment. This turned him into an unthinking machine.

'The army was also neither organized nor trained to fight a major war against an enemy armed with modern weapons – in short: the British soldier could march better than he could shoot.'

NOTES:

Ian Hamilton's March, Churchill's sequel to *London to Ladysmith via Pretoria*, was well under way, to complete his South Africa Saga.

1900	JUNE	2000
Tuesday • One VC • Boer attack repulsed near Senekal • Enemy's laager burned	**26**	Monday
Wednesday • Attack on British at Roodeval Spruit • Boers beaten off	**27**	Tuesday
Thursday • Coke in action at Graskop • Clements starts north	**28**	Wednesday
Friday • De Wet retires with his commandos to the ridges east and south-east of Lindley	**29**	Thursday
Saturday • Bethlehem still untaken *'Khaki drill when wet in the presence of a breeze acts as a refrigerator, and in later operations during the campaign the authorities have appreciated this fact, and have stopped the issue of that material, substituting serge in its place.'* – DR BLAKE KNOX	**30**	Friday

England's Dead

But let the angry sun
From Heaven look fiercely red,
Unfelt by those whose task is done
There slumber England's dead!

'That Silent Death' ...

The rattle of Mausers swelled and was maintained as one roar from within 600 yards.

As we neared the top we could hear that our men were nearby, for we had no difficulty in distinguishing the double report of the Mauser from the single crack of the English Lee Metfords.

Deneys Reitz

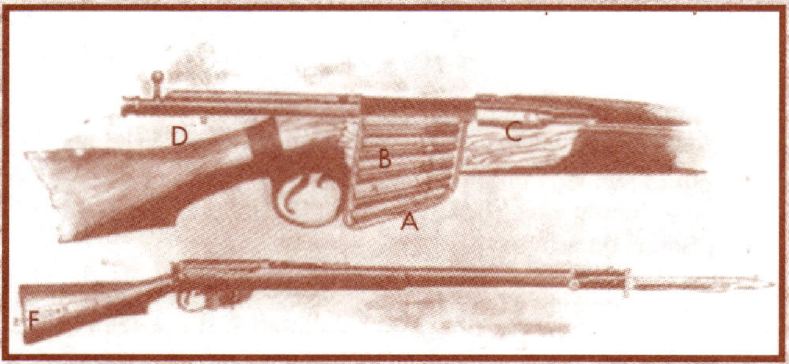

Lee-Enfield rifle, used by the British troops
The cartridges (B) are placed singly in the magazine (A), from which a spring at the bottom forces them upwards till one of them enters the breech, when it is pushed forward by the bolt (D) into the chamber (C) and fired. The withdrawal of the bolt ejects the spent cartridge. There is a slide which, when required, cuts off the magazine and allows single cartridges to be used. (F) is a cleaner and oil-can carried within the butt.

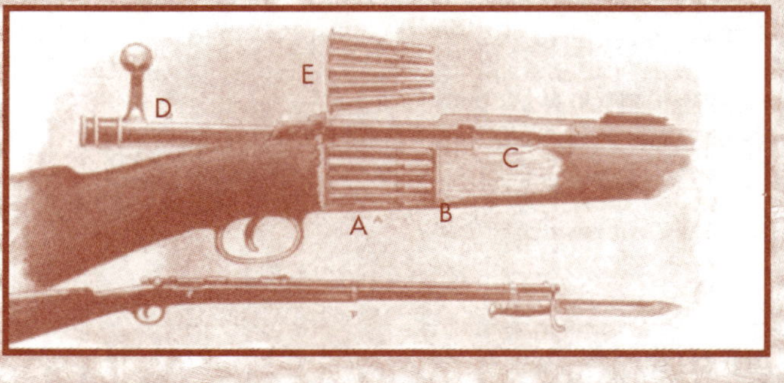

Mauser rifle, used by the Boers
The cartridges (E) are carried in a holder, from which, by one pressure of the thumb, they are released and dispose themselves in proper order in the magazine (A). They are pressed upwards by a spring (B), and forced, one at a time, into the chamber (C) by the bolt (D). The rifle is sometimes provided with a bayonet, but this the Boers do not carry.

'The Mauser and Lee Metford are what I would call humane bullets. I have seen cases where they have gone through the abdomen, the lungs and other organs of the body; and one case in which the bullet must have pierced the heart muscle but missed the cavities; and yet these cases recovered frequently; and wounds through the joints rarely resulted in amputation.'

On the other hand experience showed that Martini bullet wounds through the lungs or intestines were generally fatal, and wounds through the knee and ankle-joints generally demanded amputation. He did not believe the theory that the high velocity of the Lee-Metford bullet passing through the air heated it to such an extent as to sterilise it ... 'I am inclined to attribute its merciful qualities rather to the smallness of the bore, because I have seen small-bore revolver bullet wounds through lungs, liver and intestines recover with conservative treatment and these are low-velocity bullets.'

Fighting Mac

Hector MacDonald at Majuba

When the Gordon Highlanders were beaten back on the disastrous day of Majuba, Lieutenant MacDonald, still unwounded, rallied his men for a last stand. He was disarmed, but met the onslaught of a group of Boers with his fists, knocking down three of the enemy in succession. His pluck was appreciated. A Boer who had felt the weight of his blows called to one of his fellows, who was in the act of covering MacDonald with his rifle, to 'spare that brave man.' He was spared, and of course taken prisoner; but General Joubert treated him with consideration, even returning to him his sword – the sword which had but recently been presented to him by his fellow officers at Kandahar.

1900	JULY	2000
Sunday • Clements joins Paget at Lindley • Hunter and MacDonald join forces at Frankfort	1	Saturday
Monday • Clery at Greylingstad	2	Sunday

Arthur Richardson:

First man to win a VC while serving with a Canadian Unit under British Command

VC

Arthur Richardson: Sergeant: Lord Strathcona's Horse, Canadian Forces
Gazetted 14 September 1900
5 July 1900: Wolvespruit, Standerton: A party of Lord Strathcona's Horse (38 in number) came into contact and was engaged at close quarters with a force of 80 of the enemy. When the order was given to retire, Sergeant Richardson rode back under very heavy cross-fire, picked up a trooper whose horse had been shot and who was badly wounded and rode with him out of fire. This act of gallantry was performed within 300 yds of the enemy and Sergeant Richardson was himself riding a wounded horse.

Lieutenant.-General Sir Archibald Hunter, K.C.B., D.S.O.

Was born in 1856 in London; educated at Glasgow Academy and at Sandhurst; joined the 4th King's Own Royal Lancashires, 1874; Captain, 1882; Major, 1885; Lieutenant-Colonel 1889; Colonel, 1894; Major-General, 1896; served in the Nile expedition, 1884-5, with the Egyptian Army; with the Egyptian Frontier Field Force, 1885-6; in the operations on the Sudan frontier, 1889.

In command of a brigade in the Egyptian Army; and with the Dongola Expeditionary Force under Sir H. Kitchener in 1896 in command of the Infantry Division; in 1898 he commanded a division of the Egyptian Army at the Battle of the Atbara, and the Infantry Division at the Battle of Khartoum; Governor of Omdurman, 1899; commanded a first-class district in India, 1899; joined Sir G. White at Durban to act as his Chief-of-the-Staff until Sir Redvers Buller took command. He was promoted to local rank of Lieutenant-General and the command of the 10th Division in South Africa, March, 1900. One noteworthy feat since accomplished by General Hunter was the capture of Prinsloo and his 4,000 burghers in the Brandwater Basin.

It is a complex character, with multitudinous lights and shades, so subtle and yet so marked, that they are difficult to define accurately. But, regarding one fact, all writers of practical experience are inclined to agree that the Boer of the past was a very much finer fellow than the Boer of the present - finer morally and practically; and that in his obstinate determination to resist the march of progress he has allowed himself to suffer deterioration

LOUIS CRESWICK: *SOUTH AFRICA AND THE TRANSVAAL WAR* 1900.

'MAJUBA WAS TO COST US 20 000 LIVES TWENTY YEARS LATER AND FIGURE AS A SORT OF BUNKER HILL IN AFRIKANDER HISTORY FOR ALL TIME.' – IH

LORD ROBERTS: 'THE SOLDIERS ADORE HIM. THERE IS NEVER THE SLIGHTEST MURMUR AGAINST HIM; HE IS EVER COURTEOUS, KIND AND CONSIDERATE, AND WITHAL FIRM AS A ROCK.'

1900	JULY	2000
Tuesday • Paget in action at Baken Kop, near Lindley	**3**	Monday
Wednesday • Roberts and Buller join hands at Vlakfontein • Entire railway from Natal to Johannesburg in British hands • Carrington's 2nd Brigade arrives at Bulawayo	**4**	Tuesday
Thursday • One VC • Paget the first to come in front of Bethlehem – Clements, arriving that evening, obliged to cross to left flank	**5**	Wednesday
Friday • Clements and Paget attack De Wet at Bethlehem	**6**	Thursday
Saturday • Capture of Bethlehem • Hunter reaches Reitz • Instructions issued warning persons against harbouring rebels • Buller arrives at Pretoria	**7**	Friday
Sunday • Bruce Hamilton left at Reitz with three battalions and ten guns to guard surplus stores	**8**	Saturday
Monday • Hunter at Bethlehem	**9**	Sunday

4 JULY: CHURCHILL BOARDS THE *DUNOTTAR CASTLE* – THE SHIP THAT HAD BROUGHT HIM TO SOUTH AFRICA – AND SAILS FOR HOME.

The Gordon Highlanders

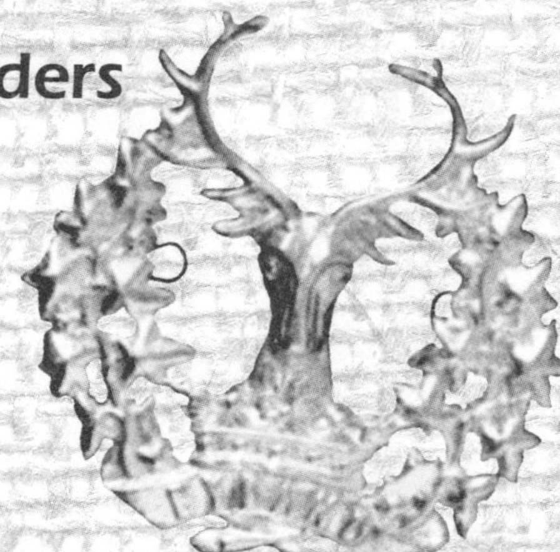

Men who desired that their honour and the honour of thier corps should be vindicated: The Majuba Action is the most notable incident in the history of the regiment, and its offficial records state that ...

'The grossest misrepresentation has prevailed about the details of the action itself, and the cause which led to its disastrous result.'

The finish of a forced march

The Highlanders here represented formed part of the reinforcements sent to General Ian Hamilton after his recapture of the Bloemfontein Waterworks, and the photograph was taken as they joined his command.

THE IDLER – *NATAL MERCURY*

Och ouch!
Shooting, and the accuracy thereof, sparks another memory. A Scottish regiment, resplendent in kilts and sporrans, found that the latter item of traditional dress provided Boer marksmen with an irresistible target.

So the Jocks are reputed to have covered their sporrans with a cloth to disguise them, but the wind uncovered the "bullseyes" and the rifle-fire rang out again.

Those incidents must have given rise to the age-old Scottish question: 'Is anything worn under the kilt?'

To which the answer is: 'Worn? Completely shot is more like it!'

VC

David Younger: Cape 1st Battalion: The Gordon Highlanders: *Gazetted 8 Aug 1902*
11 July 1900: Near Krugersdorp: Captain Younger took out a party which successfully dragged an artillery waggon under cover of a small kopje, though exposed to very heavy and accurate enemy fire. He also accompanied a second party who went out to try to bring in the guns, but during the afternoon he was mortally wounded, dying shortly afterwards.

VC

William Gordon: Captain (later Colonel) 1st Battalion: The Gordon Highlanders: *Gazetted 28 Sept 1900*
11 July 1900: Near Krugersdorp: A party of men had succeeded in dragging an artillery waggon under cover when its horses were unable to do so, because of heavy and accurate firing by the enemy. Captain Gordon then went out alone to the nearest gun under heavy fire and then having fastened a drag rope to the gun, he called for volunteers to come and help. While the gun was being moved, however, a Captain and three men were hit, and to save further casualties, Captain Gordon ordered the remainder of the party to take cover, and having seen the wounded safely away, he himself retired.

'THE BITTERNESS AFTER MAJUBA WAS INTENSE AND IN SOUTH AFRICA THE WORD IS STILL AS POISONOUS TO HANDLE AS A PUFF-ADDER.' – IH

1900	JULY	2000
Tuesday • Rundle moves out to Biddolphberg to assist Clements	**10**	Monday
Wednesday • Two VCs • Actions of Zilikat's Nek, Onderste Poort and Dwarsvlei • French and Hutton compel Boers to retire from the Tigerfontein ridge	**11**	Tuesday
Thursday *'The net was now in position and about to be drawn tight to catch the biggest fish of all.'*	**12**	Wednesday
Friday • Hunter's information: Bethlehem commando under Prinsloo now at Naauwpoort Nek with eight guns	**13**	Thursday
Saturday • Paget to go to Slabbert's Nek • Bruce Hamilton to go to Naauwpoort	**14**	Friday
Sunday • Steyn and De Wet escape from the Brandwater Basin	**15**	Saturday
Monday • De Wet engaged with Paget and Broadwood • Hutton in action at Witpoort	**16**	Sunday

To Winston Churchill:
Dilkusha
Panchagani
17 July 1944

Dear Prime Minister

You are reported to have the desire to crush the 'naked fakir', as you are said to have described me. I have been long trying to be a fakir and that, naked – a more difficult task. I therefore regard the expression as a compliment though unintended. I approach you then as such and ask you to trust and use me for the sake of your people and mine and through them those of the world.

Your sincere friend,
M.K. Gandhi

Stretcher bearers: '... On the next rise were corteges of stretcher bearers extending over a distance of three of four miles. It was indescribably ghastly and heart-rending, and made me faint and sick at heart. I witnessed the passing away of two brave souls under fearful agony. Their bearers tenderly laid them down by the roadside.

Some of the wounded were smoking their pipes in their endeavour to alleviate the pain, but the distortion on their faces showed that the relief was slight.'

Loyalty of Natal Indians: Mention should be made of the patriotic action of the Indian Community of Natal. In a colony where the Indian indentured 'coolie' is regarded as a necessary evil, and the Indian trader as an unmitigated nuisance, there seemed no special reason for the Indian community to be demonstratively exuberant in its patriotism. Some of the more far-seeing Indians, including Mr Gandhi, a lawyer whose persistent advocacy of Indian interests had brought him no little unpopularity, saw that now was an opportunity for justifying their demands for privilege by giving an example of patriotic duty. About a hundred of the leading Indians of Durban met towards the end of October and offered their services to the Government as unpaid ambulance assistants. The offer was eventually accepted and a volunteer ambulance corps, nearly 1 000 strong, was formed, which arrived at the front in time to help with the wounded of Colenso, and proved itself of great use after Spioenkop. In addition to this the Indian community undertook to look after all the Indian refugees from the Transvaal, and collected subscriptions and presents for the sick and wounded.

Leo Amery

1900	JULY	2000
Tuesday • Hunter sends empty wagons to Winburg with an escort from Paget's force	**17**	Monday
Wednesday • Roberts sends Hickman along the Magaliesberg and Methuen to Rustenburg	**18**	Tuesday
Thursday • General Little engages De Wet near Lindley and breaks up his forces	**19**	Wednesday
Friday • Hunter makes first real move on the mountains • Harrismith and Vrede commandos ten miles north-east of Golden Gate	**20**	Thursday
Saturday • Advance of Lord Roberts to Komati Poort begins • Bruce Hamilton captures Spitzkrans • Methuen forces Olifant's Nek • Attack on post at Zuikerbosch repulsed • De Wet crosses the railway at Serfontein	**21**	Friday
Sunday • Lemmer attacks 300 Bushmen under Colonel Airey near Selons River • Coke captures Graskop	**22**	Saturday
Monday • Roberts advances towards Middelburg • Broadwood in action with De Wet at Stinkhoutboom	**23**	Sunday

Neville Howse

First to win a VC while serving with an Australian Unit

VC

Neville Howse: Captain: NSW Medical Staff Corps: Australian Forces
Gazetted 4 June 1901
24 July 1900: During the action at Vredefort, Captain Howse saw a trumpeter fall and went through very heavy cross-fire to rescue the man. His horse was soon shot from under him but the Captain continued on foot, reached the casualty and dressed his wound. He then carried him to safety.

Major-General Bruce Meade Hamilton

(No relation to Ian but brother-in-law to Colley)

In command of the 21st Brigade, South Africa Field Force, with rank of Major-General. Was born in 1857, son of the late General H. Meade Hamilton, C.B. He joined the 15th Foot (afterwards the East Yorkshire regiment) in 1877; Captain, 1886; Major, 1895; Brevet Lieutenant.-Colonel, 1896; Brevet Colonel, 1897. He served with the 15th Regiment in the Afghan War in 1880; in the Boer War of 1881 as ADC to his brother-in-law, Sir George Colley, being present in the engagement at the Ingogo River, and afterwards as ADC to Sir Evelyn Wood; joined the Burmese Expedition in 1885, and the Ashanti Expedition under Sir Francis Scott in 1895 (Brevet of Lieut.-Colonel); he was with the Benin Expedition in 1897 in command of the Niger Coast Protectorate Force (Brevet of Colonel). He went out in the present war as Chief of the Staff to General Clery, and distinguished himself under General Smith-Dorrien in the fighting before Johannesburg.

'BRUCE WAS A BRAVE SOLDIER' – IH

1900	JULY	2000
Tuesday • One VC • De Wet reaches Reitzburg • Capture of Retief's and Slabbert's Neks • Howard captures Rooikoppies	24	Monday
Wednesday • Boers flee in disorder before Lord Roberts' advance at Balmoral • French crosses Oliphant's River	25	Tuesday
Thursday • Capture of Naauwpoort Nek • Hunter occupies Fouriesburg • Philip de Wet, younger brother of Christiaan de Wet, surrenders at Kroonstad	26	Wednesday
Friday • Occupation of Middelburg by advance guard of Lord Roberts	27	Thursday
Saturday • Capture of Slaapkranz Nek • Bruce Hamilton to Golden Gate	28	Friday
Sunday • Reinforcements ordered by Hunter to assist Hamilton arrive when fighting nearly over • Prinsloo sends in request for armistice – refused	29	Saturday
Monday • Surrender of Prinsloo and 4 000 Boers to General Hunter in the Brandwater Basin	30	Sunday

Prinsloo's surrender:

One of the greatest military achievements of the war.

July 30, 1900:

Scene of the surrender in the Brandwater Basin

'The great majority of the burghers, only too glad to be relieved of the intolerable strain of the last month since they had first begun to be harried by Clements and Paget, surrendered willingly. On the morning of July 30 General Hunter received the surrender of Generals Prinsloo and Crowther and of the Ficksburg and Ladybrand commandos on the appropriately named farm *Verliesfontein*. The surrendering Boers came up between the lines of the post of honour, handing over rifles and ammunition, in the case of the burghers to private soldiers, in the case of the principal officers to the General in command. There came men of all ages – even boys and old grandfathers – all well armed and well horsed. They had fought well, and now saw no other way of avoiding annihilation; their last remaining anxiety was that they should not be sent to St Helena.

It was some time before all the surrenders had come in, and many Boers, even after the majority of their fellows had handed in their arms, lurked about in the caves and recesses of the Basin, of the Langberg, and away in the adjoining long valley called Witzie's Hoek. Several of these were brought out and large stocks of ammunition were destroyed by parties of Yeomanry sent out during the ensuing weeks. Altogether, as a result of the operations, by August 9, 4 314 men had surrendered, three guns (two of them belonging to 'U' Battery) were given in, and the English captured 2 800 cattle, 4 000 sheep, 5 000 or 6 000 good horses, and destroyed nearly 2 000 000 rounds of ammunition.' – LA

NOTES:

'OF THE BEST MARKSMEN IN THE WORLD.' – WSCH

1900	JULY	2000
Tuesday	31	Monday
• Boers surrendered 2300 horses and 3 guns – 2 of which were our own		

The Marksman and the Rider

'Take a community of Dutchmen of the type of those who defended themselves for fifty years against all the power of Spain at a time when Spain was the greatest power in the world. Intermix with them a strain of those inflexible French Huguenots, who gave up their name and fortune and left their country forever at the time of the Revocation of the Edict of Nantes. The product must obviously be one of the most rugged, virile, unconquerable races ever seen upon earth. Take these formidable people and train them for seven generations in constant warfare against savage men and ferocious beasts, in circumstances in which no weakling could survive: place them so that they acquire skill with weapons and in horsemanship, give them a country which is imminently suited to the tactics of the huntsman, the marksman and the rider. Then, finally put a fine temper upon their military qualities by a dour fatalistic Old Testament religion and an ardent and consuming patriotism. Combine all these qualities and all these impulses in one individual and you have the modern Boer.'

SIR ARTHUR CONAN DOYLE (RAMBLERS' HOSPITAL, BLOEMFONTEIN)

Khaki in the British Army

There has been a good lot of correspondence lately about the date of the first issue of Khaki uniform to the British Army in India. Here, writing home at the end of 1874, it will be noticed that the word khaki is not used as it would have been ten years later and that I speak of 'snuff-coloured kit.

Ian Hamilton

Oxford Dictionary: dust-coloured; dull brownish-yellow: khaki fabric of twilled cotton or wool, used esp. in military dress: Persian word for dust

VC

William House: Private (later Lance-corporal) 2nd Battalion: The Royal Berkshire Regiment
Gazetted 7 Oct 1902

2 August 1900: Mosilikatse Nek: When a sergeant who had gone forward to reconnoitre was wounded, Private House rushed out from cover (although cautioned not to do so as the fire from the enemy was very hot) picked up the wounded sergeant and tried to bring him into shelter. In doing this he was severely wounded, but he warned his comrades not to come to his assistance as the fire was so heavy.

It is hard to understand how men, handicapped by ox-transport, whose rate of advance never exceeded 4 miles an hour, could have successfully outwitted and out-manoeuvred ten times their number converging from all sides.

An interesting reflection is that had the aeroplane been invented fifteen years earlier the whole guerrilla resistance would have been impossible. Even a handful of planes would have sufficed to spot Boer ox-convoys and bomb them.

I always invite criticism from friends before I write or do anything important. It is very much better to have one's weak points indicated by friendly critics before one acts, rather than by hostile critics when it is too late to alter.

Lord Cromer

1900	AUGUST	2000
Wednesday • Oliver, with 1500 men and several guns, breaks away from the captured force and escapes through the hills	**1**	**Tuesday**
Thursday • One VC • Ian Hamilton recaptures Zilikat's Nek • Mr Chamberlain outlines system of government of new colonies	**2**	**Wednesday**
Friday • In his official report, French remarks that he regards Oliver's escape as a dishonourable breach of faith	**3**	**Thursday**
Saturday • Colonel Hore besieged at Elands' River • MacDonald captures Harrismith	**4**	**Friday**
Sunday • Carrington driven off by Lemmer in attempting to relieve Hore	**5**	**Saturday**
Monday • De Wet enters the Transvaal having come out of his lair	**6**	**Sunday**

Brian Lawrence: Sergeant (later Lieutenant-Colonel) 17th Lancers: *Gazetted 15 Jan 1901*
7 August 1900: Near Essenbosch Farm: Sergeant Lawrence and a private were attacked by a group of Boers. The private's horse was shot and the man thrown, dislocating his shoulder. Sergeant Lawrence at once went to his assistance, put him on his own horse and sent him on to the picket. He then took the soldier's carbine, and with his own as well, kept the enemy off until the wounded man was safely out of range. The sergeant then retired for some two miles on foot, followed by the Boers, keeping them off until help arrived.

In retrospect:

Initial success turns into humiliating defeat
Majuba (1881) and Spioenkop (1900):
Colley and Buller

'The same crass fumbling by an English commander, who yet somehow still retained the confidence of his men after two badly conducted battles, turned initial success into humiliating defeat. After failing to pierce a Boer entrenched position with a frontal assault, a hilltop which commanded it was seized without loss following a bold night march. The neglect to dig proper trenches and the failure to grasp the tactical significance of the hill's natural defences were then faithfully repeated on SpioenKop. Tactically both battles were lost because of the English troops' poor shooting, and the skilful use the Boers made of cover during a counter-attack. Each action ended with the hill in Boer hands after the English had suffered heavy and absurdly disproportionate casualties. General Buller at SpioenKop, in fact, made every mistake Colley had committed on Majuba. The only difference was that Buller lived to blame them all on someone else. His failure was all the more ironical because Buller had been one of the most scathing of Sir George's critics, and when discussing Colley's inexperience of South Africa's "infernal hills" had chortled in words whose memory must afterwards have often returned to make him wince:

"He'll climb one of them, but ... won't understand that the top's no use unless you know which ridge to guard."

OLIVER RANSFORD

Spioenkop was undoubtedly the key to the Boer positions, but to use a key in order to open the door just wide enough to get one's hand in, and then to leave it there, is deliberately to invite having one's fingers crushed.

Leo Amery

'Recommendations for the VC appear to have been made on the spot at Colenso, 15 December 1899. Congreve (whose son was also to win the Cross in WW1), Reed, and Corporal Nurse were all gazetted on 2 February 1900, and even though he died within 36 hours after the action, Lieutenant Freddie Roberts was also gazetted. Since his father, Lord Roberts, had just been appointed Commander-in-Chief of the British forces in South Africa, it seems likely that the War Office felt able to bend the rules without misgivings. From 1900 onwards it was tacitly acknowledged that the VC could be awarded to men who died winning it. A Royal Warrant of 1920 eventually gave official recognition to what had long been established practice.'

Digby-Jones, RE; Albrecht, ILH; Atkinson, YR and Younger, GH, were the first Posthumous VC's – all gazetted 8 Aug 1902.

'FAILURE TO DIG IN: A CRIME, NOT SO MUCH AGAINST THE SCIENCE OF WAR AS AGAINST THE ART OF WAR.' – IH

'WHATEVER BULLER DID WAS DONE THOROUGHLY AND ON SOUND PRINCIPLE.'

1900	AUGUST	2000
Tuesday • One VC • Buller occupies Amersfoort	**7**	Monday
Wednesday • Olivier is re-captured but not court-martialled for his breach of the rules of war – perhaps the Empire is too quick to let bygones be bygones	**8**	Tuesday
Thursday • Utmost difficulty in getting supplies to large bodies of troops so far from the Cape base • Methuen on the heels of De Wet	**9**	Wednesday
Friday • De Wet crosses the Gatsrand • Discovery of the plot at Pretoria to kidnap Lord Roberts and British Officers	**10**	Thursday
Saturday • De Wet succeeds in crossing the railway line near Welverdiend • Army base shifted from Cape to Durban, the distance shortened by two-thirds – the army on the railway instead of hundreds of miles from it	**11**	Friday
Sunday • Methuen captures wagons and prisoners from De Wet • Buller reaches Ermelo	**12**	Saturday
Monday • Army base in Durban assures Lord Robert's communications from serious attack and enabled him to consolidate his position in Pretoria	**13**	Sunday

'MARK – AND REMEMBER FOR THE REST OF YOUR LIVES – THAT TOMMY ATKINS MADE NO DISTINCTION BETWEEN THE WOUNDED ENEMY AND HIS DEAREST FRIEND.' – GS

Kitchener

His attitude towards a meddlesome correspondent

Churchill's criticism of Kitchener in his book *The River War*, directly led to soldiers not doubling up as correspondents, hence his resignation from the 4th Hussars in order to come to SA as a journalist for *The Morning Post*. Buller bent this rule after Churchill's escape from Pretoria, on condition that he did not draw army pay. Retaining his rank as 2nd Lieutenant, he joined the 'Sakabula's': The South African Light Horse.

16 September 1898:
Winston's letter to Hamilton after Omdurman:

I am in great disfavour with the authorities here. Kitchener was furious with Sir E. Wood for sending me out and expressed himself freely. My remarks on the treatment of the wounded – again disgraceful – were repeated to him and generally things have been a little unpleasant. ...

A great character marred by a mass of foibles and tricks...

The fact that he should have vanished at the very moment Winston and I were making out an unanswerable case against him was one of those coups with which his career was crowded – he was not going to answer! He had always had a horror of cold water, and the shock of the icy sea would at once extinguish his life.

A Royal Commission on the Dardanelles'... seemed, to the Government, yielding to parliamentary pressure, the lesser of two evils, for publication of the Dardanelles' documents would have shown up Lord K with altogether too bright a searchlight beam and put them in a hole... because they must give away Lord K, if the story is fairly told. The tragedy of the 'Hampshire' simply precludes publication at present.'

I. Hamilton

Lord Kitchener drowned when HMS *Hampshire* struck a mine.

Roberts gave up the command at the end of 1900, to be succeeded by Kitchener. Kitchener had his own reasons for ending the war as soon as he could; he wished to be given the post of Commander-in-Chief in India, which he feared would elude him if he could not end the campaign in South Africa quickly; he was not concerned with the political consequences of his actions; rapidly his regard for Milner deteriorated into indifference, Milner's for him into mistrust. In military operations it seemed that the British army had lost the initiative, and was compelled, in innumerable local actions, to react to Boer movements. General Christiaan de Wet made two spectacular raids, in which he slipped through superior British forces and made his escape. Militarily, De Wet's operations achieved little that was lasting, but they did demonstrate the inability of the British army either to catch or to force a commando to battle against its will.

1900	AUGUST	2000
Tuesday • De Wet escapes through Olifant's Nek • Strathcona's Horse enter Carolina	14	Monday
Wednesday • Buller reaches Twyfelaar	15	Tuesday
Thursday • Lord Kitchener relieves Hore at Elands' River • Martial law withdrawn from Molteno district	16	Wednesday
Friday • De Wet appears at Commando Nek on the little Crocodile River • Baden-Powell summoned to surrender	17	Thursday
Saturday • De Wet swings eastward and endeavours to cross to the north of Pretoria	18	Friday
Sunday • De Wet heard of at Hebron • Steyn sent on with a small escourt	19	Saturday
Monday • De Wet turns back to the Free State – Baden-Powell and Paget having blocked his path	20	Sunday

VC

Henry Knight: Corporal (later Captain) 1st Battalion: The King's (Liverpool) Regiment
Gazetted 4 Jan 1901
21 Aug 1900: During operations near Van Wyk's Vlei, Corporal Knight and four men were covering the right rear of a detachment of their company when they were attacked by the enemy. The corporal held his ground, directing his men to retire one by one to better cover, where he maintained his position for nearly an hour, covering the withdrawal of part of their company, and losing two of his four men. He then retired, taking with him two wounded men, one of whom he left in a place of safety and the other he carried himself for nearly two miles.

VC

Harry Hampton: Sergeant (later Colour-Sergeant) 2nd Battalion: The King's (Liverpool) Regiment
Gazetted 18 Oct 1901
21 Aug 1900: Van Wyk's Vlei: Sergeant Hampton, in command of a small party of mounted infantry, held an important position for some time against heavy odds, and when compelled to retire saw all his men into safety, although he himself had been wounded in the head. He supported a lance-corporal who was unable to walk until the latter was hit again and apparently killed. Sergeant Hampton received another wound some time later.

The plot to kidnap Lord Roberts:

'Pretoria and Johannesburg were full of Boer sympathizers, some of whom, besides giving information to the commandos, were plotting actively against the British administration. Hans Cordua, a German officer on parole, was preparing a scheme for kidnapping Lord Roberts and other officers, and at Johannesburg a plot was afoot to celebrate the taking of the Bastille on 14 July by overpowering the officers of the garrison at a race-meeting announced for that day, and then handing over the town to a commando waiting near the Crocodile River.

In Johannesburg Major Davies, through the excellent intelligence system which he had started as Chief of the Police, discovered the race-course plot in time, arrested over 400 of those principally concerned and, by Lord Roberts' orders, deported them.

**Cordua's plot at Pretoria was not discovered till a month later, when he was arrested. Cordua's attempt to get up a plot, led to one of the very few executions which were actually carried out after sentence of death imposed by a military court in the occupied territories. The originator of the plot, Hans Cordua, a young German who had come out to the Transvaal shortly before the war, had been made a lieutenant in the Transvaal forces. He was tried by a military tribunal on two charges: 1) violating his parole in two instances and 2) treacherously conspiring against British authority. The evidence produced at the trial showed that Cordua, who had been released on parole in Pretoria, had endeavoured to induce Major Erasmus, of the State Artillery, and other ex-officers and burghers to enter into a plot to kidnap Lord Roberts and other officers of the British army in Pretoria. To induce the former to join him Cordua stated that he was in communication with General Botha and the Boer commandos in the neighbourhood. The prisoner was arrested outside the outpost lines dressed in British uniform. Cordua was found guilty of both charges and sentenced to be shot. The sentence was carried into effect. Although Cordua thoroughly deserved his fate his case created great excitement among the Dutch, while the fact that he had been assisted in arranging his plot by a South American named Gano, a detective in the pay of the British, evoked considerable sympathy in England.'
– LA**

1900	AUGUST	2000
Tuesday • Two VCs • A fresh and more stringent proclamation shows that Roberts is losing patience in the face of the wholesale return of paroled men to the field – such perfidy to be severely punished in future	**21**	Monday
Wednesday • Repeated breaches of parole called imperatively for an example – Hans Cordua to be executed for his broken faith rather than for his hare-brained scheme to kidnap Roberts	**22**	Tuesday
Thursday • One VC (see page 120) • One man killed in action found to have nine signed passes in his pocket – it is against such abuses that the extra severity of the British is aimed	**23**	Wednesday
Friday • Belfast occupied by Pole-Carew • Lord Roberts leaves for Eastern Transvaal to operate against Botha	**24**	Thursday
Saturday • Roberts arrives to command his troops on the field of battle for the last time • Hans Cordua executed for conspiracy to kidnap Lord Roberts	**25**	Friday
Sunday • Commandant Olivier and his two sons captured at Winburg	**26**	Saturday
Monday • One VC (see page 120) • Battle of Bergendal: Buller defeats Botha (Dalmanutha)	**27**	Sunday

'For the second time in my life I ran from the Boers'

> *'On April 22, 1900, near Dewetsdorp, the war was raging to its climax. Winston Churchill was there and had been tipped off to expect some excitement. He got more than he bargained for and it nearly cost him his life.'*
>
> EASTERN PROVINCE HERALD 20 SEPT 1976

'British cavalry had advanced rapidly into position in front of Dewetsdorp in preparation for an attack on the koppie-ringed town.

This evidently alarmed the defenders, who had to guess whether this was to start an attack or a reconnaissance. They countered by sending a mounted party cantering across the front, from the koppie that hid Dewetsdorp, towards another, strewn with white stones.

The cavalry was supported by Montmorency's Scouts, commanded by Angus McNeil. The scouts were ready for anything, well disciplined, with good mounts and plenty of spirit. They had, however, underestimated the determination and marksmanship of the Boers.

The shining boots and smart uniforms of the British soldiers contrasted bizarrely with the appearance of the Boers in farm clothes, old coats – and on this occasion one with a red scarf vivid round his neck.

All had long beards and their reputation for being willing to fight to the last man gave them a formidably grim look.

The scene was set for action, which began with shelling by long-range British guns. When the Boer horsemen took cover behind a rise, Angus McNeil persuaded the general to let the scouts cut them off in a race for the white hill.

Some of the 50 scouts called to Winston Churchill to follow and offered him 'a first class show'. Churchill measured the distance with his eyes and decided to take the risk. All spurred their horses and the deadly dangerous race for the koppie was on.

Suddenly five well-mounted Boers leading about 200 others appeared from nowhere, then another dozen or so. Here was a new situation for McNeil to consider. He halted his troop, deciding that he could not sacrifice his scouts, now heavily outnumbered, in a contest on an open plain.

As they turned to gallop back, the Boers opened fire from the saddle. The horses plunged wildly in the whirr of bullets. Churchill was unseated and his horse galloped off. He was left standing far from cover. He ran for his life thinking (as he recorded later) "Here at last I take it."

But he saw a scout nearby, a tall man with a skull-and-crossbones badge, riding a pale horse. He shouted to him: "Give me a stirrup!".

The scout reined in for him. They did not bungle the business of mounting and rode off hard. As they seemed to fly through the air Churchill grabbed the horse's mane. His hand felt the wetness of blood. Yet the wounded horse extended itself nobly and brought both men to safety. Then it dropped and died.

Trooper Clem Roberts groaned over his beloved Rajah, the fine horse he had bred and broken himself on his farm before he joined Montmorency's Scouts.

Churchill comforted him with thanks for having saved his life. Testily Roberts brushed that away as he cried, "My poor horse, my poor, bloody horse." He cursed his ill-luck as he had expected to get away, a galloping horse being a difficult target.

The British troops who had watched the episode with excitement agreed that the scout who had stopped under fire to save a comrade had earned a distinction. The officers agreed that Trooper Roberts deserved the Victoria Cross.

The mane and tail of the horse were sent to England and eventually returned to Clem Roberts. The hair had been made into a necklace of links woven into each other by hand. A watch cord was made too.'

But evidently the authorities were not appreciative of having the Morning Post's correspondent restored to them. Trooper Roberts did not receive the Victoria Cross, nor any other distinction. Not until years later when Churchill was Secretary of State for Colonies - succeeded in obtaining for him a distinguished conduct medal, was the Trooper's bravery officially recognized.

BR

'SUIT THE ACTION TO THE WORD, THE WORD TO THE ACTION.' – SHAKESPEARE

1900	AUGUST	2000
Tuesday • Buller's troops occupy Machadodorp • Bergendal occupied	**28**	**Monday**
Wednesday • Kruger flees to Nelspruit • Boers evacuate Helvetia: occupied by Buller	**29**	**Tuesday**
Thursday • Capture of Nooitgedacht – release of 2 000 British prisoners • British occupy Waterval Boven	**30**	**Wednesday**
Friday • Humiliating, but an interesting fact that from the first to the last no fewer than 7 000 British troops passed into Boer power – all of them now recovered save some 60 officers	**31**	**Thursday**

War Wears A Double Face

One face is a mask which has been thrust upon it, and this face is all laughter;
The other is the natural face of war, and it is all tears.
The two are not seen as alternatives,
But always side by side.

JBA

William Heaton: Private (later Sergeant): 1st Battalion: The King's (Liverpool) Regiment
Gazetted 18 Jan 1901
23 Aug 1900: At Geluk, a company of the 1st Battalion: The King's (Liverpool) Regiment became surrounded by the enemy and was suffering severely. Private Heaton volunteered to take a message back to explain the position of the company and he carried out this mission successfully at imminent risk to his own life. Had it not been for his courage, the remainder of his company would almost certainly have had to surrender.

Alfred Durrant: Private (later Lance-Corporal): 2nd Battalion: The Rifle Brigade
Gazetted 18 Oct 1901
27 Aug 1900: Bergendal: A wounded and somewhat dazed corporal got up from his prone position in the firing line and started to run towards the enemy. Private Durrant rose and, pulling him down, tried to keep him quiet, but finding this impossible, took him up and carried him back for 200 yds under heavy fire to shelter. The private then returned immediately to his place in the line.

Guy Wylly: Lieutenant (later Colonel): Tasmanian Imperial Bushmen
Gazetted 23 Nov 1900
1 Sep 1900: Near Warmbaths: Lieutenant Wylly was one of the advance scouting party passing through a narrow gorge, when the enemy suddenly opened fire at close range and six out of the party of eight were wounded, including Lieutenant Wylly, who, seeing that one of his men was badly wounded in the leg and that his horse was shot, went back to him. He made the wounded man take his horse while he, the Lieutenant, opened fire from behind a rock to cover the retreat of the others, at the imminent risk of being cut off himself.

John Bisdee: Trooper (later Lieutenant-Colonel): Tasmanian Imperial Bushmen
Gazetted 12 Nov 1900
1 September 1900: Warmbaths: Transvaal: Trooper Bisdee was one of an advance scouting party passing through a narrow gorge, when the enemy suddenly opened fire at close range and six out of the party of eight were wounded, including two officers. The horse of one of the wounded officers bolted and Trooper Bisdee dismounted, put him on his own horse and took him out of range of the very heavy fire.

NOTES:

'PRIVATE MEANS HELPED A MAN TO THE TOP OF THE TREE. ROBERTS HAD NONE; BULLER HAD PLENTY.' ...

'IN WAR, THEY SAY - AND IT IS TRUE - MEN GROW CALLOUS: AN AFTERNOON OF SHOOTING AND THE LOSS OF YOUR BROTHER HURTS YOU LESS THAN A WEEK BEFORE DID A THORN IN YOUR DOG'S PAW.' – GS

'It is strange that the Afrikaner should form such close bonds with his leaders, he who to a great extent inherited the French tendency to individualism and the Dutch self-assuredness from his forebears. The Dutch blood made him headstrong and obstinate; the French disposition led him to hold views of his own on any subject under the sun and to advocate them without inhibition. In his biography on President Paul Kruger, father of the nation, J.F. de Oordt identifies the Afrikaner as someone who associated himself with persons rather than with principles. "Generally speaking", he alleges "we do not possess the powers or imagination nor sufficient philosophy to associate ourselves with something we cannot see with our own eyes. To form a distinction between a principle and a person pursuing the principle is something of which the Afrikaner has no conception".

The truth of these contentions is borne out by the old political designations such as the Botha-people, Hertzog-ites, and even Malan-ites. It is in fact true that whenever a powerful Boer personality emerged on the political front, he was soon tempted to act autocratically. We have had our strong premiers who, at times, had appropriate powers inconsistent with national interests.

PIET MEIRING 'OUR FIRST SIX PREMIERS'
(TRANSLATED FROM AFRIKAANS) JHB 1972

1900	SEPTEMBER 2000
Saturday • Two VCs • Lord Roberts proclaims the Annexation of the Transvaal • Fourie besieges Ladybrand	**1** Friday
Sunday • Buller faces heavy shell fire from the indomitable Botha at Badfontein • The days of unnecessary frontal attacks are over and Buller is forced to wait for Hamilton's column to outflank Botha's defensive position at Rietfontein	**2** Saturday
Monday • Whatever criticism directed against some episodes in the Natal campaign, it must never be forgotten that to Buller and his men have fallen some of the hardest tasks of the war	**3** Sunday

... 'THE SAME PRINCIPLE HELD LATER ON (1915) WHEN HAIG SUCCEEDED FRENCH AS C-I-C BRITISH EXPEDITIONARY FORCES.'

Guerrilla War: Misnomer

In September 1900 the Transvaal was annexed. The second phase – that of the great British-offensive – was over, and it seemed that with it the war was over. The third phase of the war lasted another eighteen months. This is sometimes referred to as the guerrilla war. The phrase is a misnomer. A guerrilla war is carried out by small bodies of irregular troops, acting independently. The Boer armies had been defeated in the field, they had been dispersed; but they had not been broken. The Boer governments had been dislodged from their capitals; but, peripatetic though their existence was, they retained their authority. President Kruger, an old and broken man, had sailed from Lourenço Marques for Europe, but his authority devolved upon Schalk Burger, Vice-President of the South African Republic, and was effectively shared with General Louis Botha, the Commandant-General of the Republic's forces.

Tommy and the veld peasant

'FOR THE MOST PART THEY WERE FINE TALL MEN WITH SHAGGY BEARDS, REMINDING ONE OF YORKSHIRE FARMERS, BUT ROUGHER AND NOT SO WELL DRESSED.' – HN

1900 SEPTEMBER 2000

1900	2000
Tuesday • Generals Buller and Botha engaged at Leydenburg	**4** Monday
Wednesday • Attack on Canadian post at Pan repulsed • Bruce Hamilton relieves Ladybrand	**5** Tuesday
Thursday • Buller captures Leydenburg • French occupies Carolina	**6** Wednesday
Friday *'On the pass being cleared it was found that Hamilton's march had compelled the Boers to abandon their positions in front of Buller, who had been making careful reconnaissances for a joint attack from the front.'*	**7** Thursday
Saturday • Buller drives the Boers under Botha from Paardeplaats • Spitzkop captured	**8** Friday
Sunday • Buller pushes forward to Spitzkop – rearguard resistance by Boers overpowered • Methuen scatters a Boer force at Malopo	**9** Saturday
Monday • Buller reaches Klipgat, halfway between Mauchberg and Spitzkop	**10** Sunday

The Third Phase of the War

On paper, the two Republics had been annexed, but there was no effective occupation. The third phase of the war was one of movement and attrition, in which a dwindling number of Boers maintained their resistance, hoping for a weakening of British resolution, and a large British army, constantly reinforced, lumbered about, over thousands of square miles of country, pecking away at Boer strength.

It was in this third phase of the war that the contest changed its nature; it seemed to the Boers that the British were seeking to exterminate them as a people. It became increasingly difficult for the British to distinguish between civilian and military enemies. The new pattern showed itself first in the Orange Free State, renamed the Orange River Colony on its annexation. A large number of Free Staters had surrendered, and had been permitted to return to their farms after having taken an 'oath of neutrality' – a curiously named promise to take no further part in the war. Neither President Steyn nor, later, Acting President Burger, recognized either the annexations or the right of their own people to contract out of the war. The British provided little protection for those who had surrendered; Boer commandos pounced upon them and threatened them with immediate punishment as deserters, or more remote fears of punishment by the British apostates. Roberts turned to 'farm-burning' of the homesteads of those who had broken their oaths, and a circle of reprisals began. Furthermore, 'camps of refuge', under military control, were set up in which the surrendered could take refuge with their families: this was the beginning of the system of 'concentration camps.'

NOTES:

11 September 1896: Winston Churchill, having joined the 4th Hussars at the beginning of 1895, sailed with his regiment for India where he was stationed in the Madras Province of Southern India.

1900	SEPTEMBER	2000
Tuesday • Kruger takes refuge at Lourenco Marques – the last of the old-world Puritans, he departs pouring over his well-thumbed Bible	**11**	Monday
Wednesday • The Boers stream through Burgers Pass and fling 13 of their ammunition wagons over the cliffs to prevent them from falling into the hands of the British horsemen	**12**	Tuesday
Thursday • Proclamation by Lord Roberts calling on the Boers to surrender • French occupies Barberton	**13**	Wednesday
Friday • Methuen runs down a Boer convoy and regains one of the Colenso guns and much ammunition • French releases remaining British prisoners and takes possession of 40 locomotives	**14**	Thursday
Saturday • Buller occupies Spitzkop in the north and captures a quantity of stores	**15**	Friday
Sunday • British occupy Nelspruit	**16**	Saturday
Monday • The loss of stores, and occasionally of lives, is more serious than the actual interruption of railroad traffic by the Boers	**17**	Sunday

KRUGER NEVER RETURNED TO SOUTH AFRICA BUT DIED FOUR YEARS LATER BY THE SHORES OF LAKE GENEVA.

The Imperial Light Horse 1899–1949

The origin of the movement:

Having failed in their constitutional attempts to secure a reasonable voice in the government, or any redress of their grievances, there came the time when men's thoughts naturally turned to the last expedient – force.

The Imperial Light Horse, whose Colonels-in-Chief have been successively Their Late Majesties King Edward VII and King George V, His Majesty King Edward VIII and the present King, His Majesty King George VI, was founded in Pietermaritzburg in September 1899, and has just attained its 50th Anniversary – fifty years of service during which period it has become famous for its brilliant achievements in three wars.

The founders of the Regiment had no difficulty in selecting officers and men from among the large number of volunteers who came forward. The original strength was 500 officers and men and those selected from 5000 who volunteered.

The command was given to Colonel J.J. Scott Chisholme, who was seconded from the 5th Royal Irish Lancers. The first Adjutant was Lieutenant Reginal Barnes of the 4th Hussars (later Major-General Sir Reginal Barnes, KCB, DSO).

After only one month's training the Regiment distinguished itself at the battle of Elandslaagte where it suffered heavy losses, including Colonel J.J. Scott Chisholme, the Commanding Officer.

The Regiment, with the exception of one squadron which later joined the relieving force, next earned distinction in the Siege of Ladysmith. Then followed the Relief of Mafeking and the March on Pretoria, and later hard fighting in the Western Transvaal and the Free State, the Regiment being in the field until the end of the war.

A Battle with Kitchener for I.L.H. Recognition

'Roberts was sympathetic and courteous and was shocked and moved when told of the treatment given to colonial units like the I.L.H. They knew the country and the enemy, had initiative, resourcefulness and steadiness, and Kitchener also admitted that as horsemen, marksmen and masters of veld-craft they were invaluable. Yet despatches praising them were not published, and recommendations for decorations were ignored. At Elandslaagte, for instance, the I.L.H. had helped the Gordons out of a tight corner and General French had recommended awards for gallantry, including two VC's. These were, however, passed over, though at least two Gordons received the coveted medal. Roberts asked Percy Fitzpatrick to draft a report on these and other grievances. Now Kitchener disliked Milner and Milner's men, hence was "hard as the hinges of Hades" with Fitzpatrick. But Fitzpatrick took his own way, gave up the polite approach and "laid into the war-lord", the straighter, the better he panned out and thus conceded most of the points. Two VC's were awarded to the regiment.'

J.P.R. Wallis

I.L.H.: Nobody who knew them can ever forget them. To have seen them fight, to have held, as I always did, the steadfast faith in their courage and discipline, will, to my dying day, remain a cherished remembrance.

Sir Archibald Hunter

I.L.H.: Imperium et Libertas:
Empire and Liberty: clearly expressing the purpose and origin of the Regiment

Buller's mishandling of colonial irregulars like the I.L.H. drove Woolls-Sampson to blaze out: 'Tell me, Fitz, is the man a bloody traitor or a bloody fool?'

1900	SEPTEMBER	2000
Tuesday • Boers forced out of Hornies Nek 10 miles north of Pretoria • Rundle captures a gun at Bronkhorstfontein	**18**	Monday
Wednesday • British Generals busy stamping out the remaining embers of what had been so terrible a conflagration	**19**	Tuesday
Thursday • British occupy Kaap Muiden	**20**	Wednesday
Friday • Roberts returns to Pretoria	**21**	Thursday
Saturday • Settle relieves Schweizer Reneke	**22**	Friday
Sunday • Much trouble but no great damage inflicted on British during incessant attacks on railway lines by roving bands of Boers	**23**	Saturday
Monday • Pole-Carew reaches KomatiPoort • Evacuation of all Boer positions near Portuguese frontier	**24**	Sunday

'It was murder, sheer absolute murder.'

– Lord Roberts

Lieutenant the Honourable Frederick High Sherton Roberts, V.C.

'The Queen has been graciously pleased to signify her intention to confer the decoration of the Victoria Cross on the undermentioned officer, whose name has been submitted for Her Majesty's approval, for his conspicuous bravery at the Battle of Colenso.'

But in the moment of victory Lieutenant Roberts fell mortally wounded, and died a few hours later, to the inexpressible grief of the whole British Empire.

'Rarely does a young officer take up duty with a British regiment under more favourable auspices than did young Freddy. To be the son and grandson of a distinguished soldier is, in itself, considered a recommendation for the profession of arms, but of Lieut. Roberts it can be fairly said that he was the only son of the most popular soldier of his generation – Field-Marshal Lord Roberts of Kandahar, V.C. 'Our only other General'. Modest and unassuming, he made friends on all sides, and is an undoubted acquisition, but burning to receive his 'baptism of fire'.

When the staff was being formed for the South African Field Force he was offered by Sir Redvers Buller the post of Aide-de-camp on his personal Staff and as such he landed at Cape Town. Accompanying Sir Redvers afterwards to Natal, he had the misfortune to lose his life in the first action for the relief of Ladysmith, on December 15th, 1899, in circumstances of exceptional sadness, seeing he was struck down at the very moment when he had so honourably won the decoration which, beyond all others, a brave soldier treasures —the Cross 'for Valour'.

The only surviving son: … 'A few days later the rewards for the expedition were published and he (Lord Roberts) found himself gazetted a brevet lieutenant-colonel. And almost at the same time a baby girl was born, and christened Evelyn Sautelle. Indeed he had reason to be happy.

In January 1869 the family set sail once more on the next lap of life's journey. It was to be the most eventful of them all and nearly thirteen years were to elapse before they saw England again …

They had a sad trip out, for the little girl of whom they were so proud died and was buried in the Red Sea. Then back in Simla, where they spent a very quiet year, a boy was born, who only lived three weeks. They had now been married ten years, yet still had no children and at times were almost in despair. But in September 1870 a girl arrived to be followed by a boy in 1872 and another girl three years later, so faith and courage were well rewarded in the end.

September 1904: Lord and Lady Roberts and their two surviving daughters, accompanied by Major Furse as ADC, went on a three months' tour of South Africa. After visiting the Victoria Falls, Bulawayo, Mafeking, Kimberley and Bloemfontein, they toured 'Buller's Battlefields'. A small incident of pathetic significance occurred when Roberts himself and Furse were alone together, looking from a height at the battlefield of Colenso. After a few minutes of dead silence, Roberts turned impulsively to his companion and remarked: 'It was murder, sheer absolute murder.' This was the only comment he ever allowed himself on his son's death …

1900	SEPTEMBER	2000
Tuesday • Occupation of Komati Poort • Dissolution of the British Parliament	**25**	Monday
Wednesday • The Boer cause apparently tottering to its fall – disintegration steadily setting in	**26**	Tuesday
Thursday • Schalk Burger assumes the office of Vice-President after the flight of President Kruger	**27**	Wednesday
Friday • Exiled burghers moodily pace the streets of Lourenco Marques – Kruger, his pipe dangling from his mouth, sits in the corner of the Governor's verandah	**28**	Thursday
Saturday • For the time it seems that the campaign is over – that excellent artillery which had fought so gallant a fight against our more numerous guns is found destroyed and abandoned	**29**	Friday
Sunday • Ian Hamilton at Hector Spruit finds the remains of many guns, including two of our horse artillery 12-pounders	**30**	Saturday

For six long hours every afternoon the heat of the Indian sun kept him indoors with nothing to do. He felt the need for mental stimulus: so he began to read: history, philosophy and economics: Gibbon and Macaulay, Plato and Schopenhauer, Malthus and Darwin.

BR

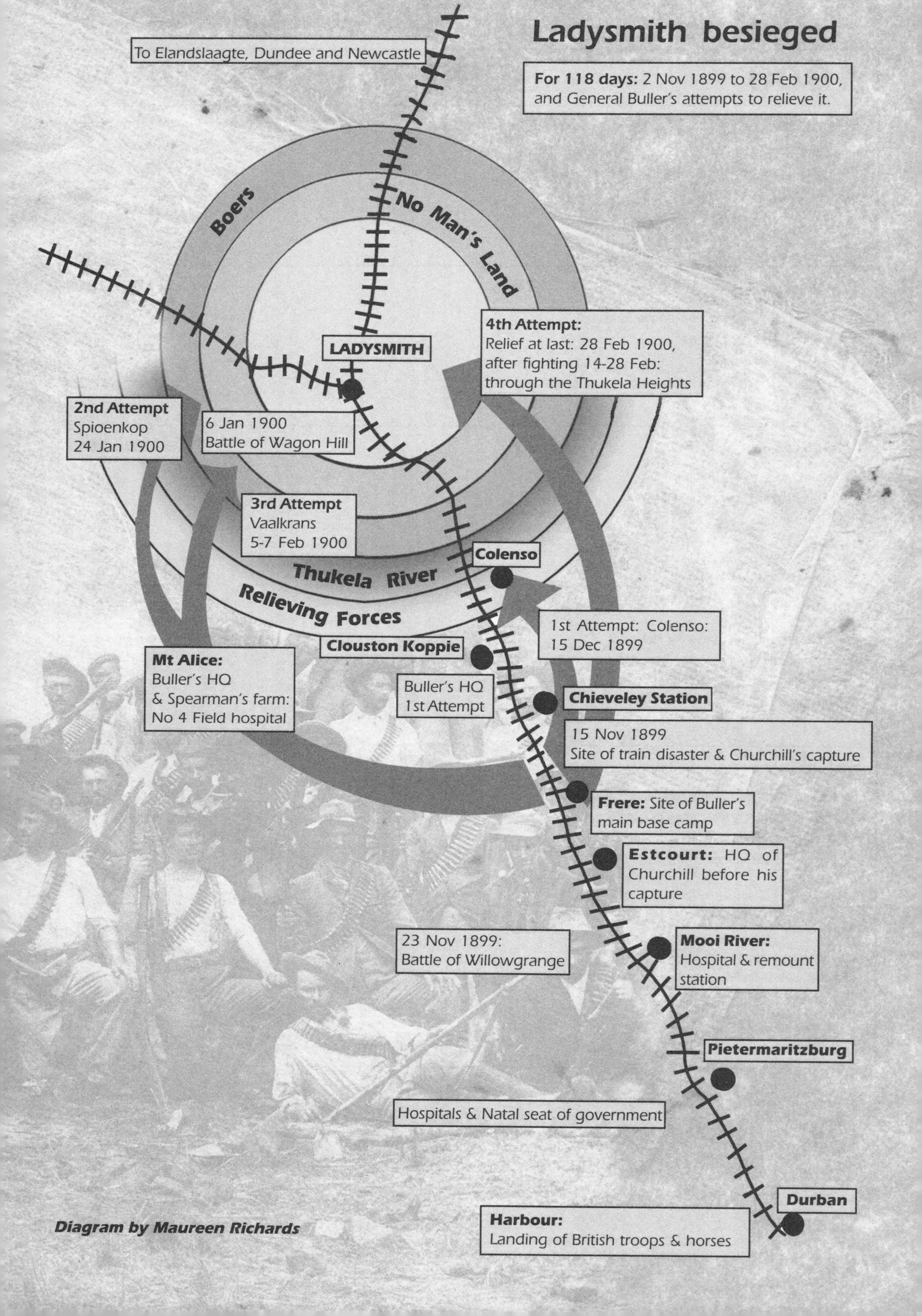

Diagram by Maureen Richards

Cameos of old Natal

Two howitzers

When the Relief of Ladysmith became a reality, the town was subjected to a veritable 'bombardment' of congratulatory telegrams and messages of goodwill. A more concrete recognition of the good fight put up by the inhabitants came from the Prime Minister of the Cape Colony, J. Gordon Sprigg. Through Sir Alfred Milner and the Governor of Natal, he asked the Ladysmith municipality whether it would be prepared to accept as a congratulatory gesture two 6.3 howitzers which had done so much in the defence of the town. These guns, with ammunition, had been issued by the Cape Colony on loan to the Imperial authorities in October 1899 after the outbreak of the Boer War and the idea was that the guns be retained as momentoes of the siege. On February 4, 1901, Councillor Christopher, seconded by Councillor Sparks, proposed that the kind offer be accepted with thanks. Thus it was that the guns came to Ladysmith in perpetuity – a now silent reminder of 120 days of siege.

To this day the 'twins', Castor and Pollux, guard the Ladysmith Town Hall.

A 5-INCH HOWITZER
Partly in section, showing the hydraulic buffers and the apparatus for raising and lowering the muzzle. This weapon can be fired at an elevation of forty-five degrees; it is intended to throw its shell high into the air so that it shall fall within the enemy's earthworks or other defences.

1900	OCTOBER	**2000**
Monday	**1**	Sunday
• Winston Churchill elected to Parliament • Rouxville threatened by a Boer force		

'Chamberlain was flexible, Milner dogmatic'

The appointment of Milner, a little known civil servant, as High Commissioner to South Africa showed Chamberlain's supreme political skill and perceptiveness:

'An executing hand has rarely been in more perfect sympathy with a directing brain' – J.S.

Sir Alfred Milner

Son of a doctor of medicine; was educated in Germany, and at King's College, London, and Balliol College, Oxford; Barrister, 1881; engaged in journalism, 1882-5; Private Secretary to Mr Goschen, 1887-9; Under Secretary for Finance in Egypt, 1889-92; Chairman of the Board of Inland Revenue, 1892-7; K.C.B., 1895; Governor of the Cape, and High Commissioner of South Africa since 1897.

1895: December 29: Jameson, leading 700 horsemen and 2 guns, started from Pitsani and crossed the Transvaal border. Boer commandos, held in readiness, easily surrounded Dr Jameson and his force, who were forced to surrender. The rebellion was quelled in Johannesburg, the leaders and millionaires concerned all arrested and delivered by the Boers to British justice; their chief and his lieutenants tried and sentenced to two years imprisonment.

The Jameson Raid

The event shook Europe and excited the whole world and Great Britain was censured in unmeasured terms in every country.

Consequences of the Jameson Raid:

1. British reputation worldwide received a grievous wound.
2. Dutch hurled Cecil Rhodes from power in Cape Colony.
3. British nation took German Emperor's telegram to President Kruger ordering German Marines who happened to be on the spot, to disembark at Delagoa Bay, as a revelation of a hostile mood.
4. The German Emperor, completely powerless in the face of British sea power, turned his mind to the construction of a German fleet.
5. The entire course of South African politics turned away from peaceful channels.
6. British colonists looked to the Imperial Government for aid.
7. The Dutch throughout the sub-continent rallied around the standards of the two Boer republics.
8. The British Government gathered themselves together after their disastrous set-back.
9. Transvaal taxed the Uitlanders all the more and began to arm heavily out of the proceeds.

'TO MILNER, THE OBJECT OF THE WAR WAS TO BREAK AFRIKANER NATIONALISM.'

1900	OCTOBER	2000
Tuesday • Expectations marking the end of the war are disappointed – South Africa is destined to be afflicted and the British Empire disturbed by a useless guerrilla campaign	**2**	Monday
Wednesday • Return of General Buller to Leydenburg	**3**	Tuesday
Thursday • After the great and dramatic events of the struggle between Briton and Boer for the mastery of South Africa, it is somewhat of an anti-climax to turn one's attention to the scattered operations to prolong the resistance for a further turbulent one and a half years	**4**	Wednesday
Friday • Barton leaves Krugersdorp to move slowly down the line of the railroad *'Although we may deplore the desperate resolution which bids brave men prefer death to subjugation, it is not for us to condemn it.'* – CD	**5**	Thursday
Saturday • Commission signed separating Office of High Commissioner from Governorship of Cape Colony, and attaching it to Sir Alfred Milner personally	**6**	Friday
Sunday *'The British had learned their lesson so thoroughly that they often turned the tables upon their instructors.'* – CD	**7**	Saturday
Monday • Sir Alfred Milner appointed administrator of new colonies	**8**	Sunday

The Ultimatum

A briefer or more arrogant ultimatum has rarely been penned in the course of history:

Sir, – In the name of the Government of the South African Republic I have the honour to bring to your information that this Government, with an eye to the breaking off of friendly relations by Her Majesty's Government, as shown by the constant bringing up of troops to the borders of this Republic, and the sending of war reinforcements from all parts of the British Empire, herewith informs you that unless they receive within forty-eight hours an assurance (1) that the troops on the borders of this Republic shall be instantly withdrawn; (2) that all reinforcements which have arrived in South Africa since June 1, 1899, shall be removed within a reasonable time; (3) that Her Majesty's troops which are now on the high seas shall not be landed in any part of South Africa – my Government will consider such action of Her Majesty's Government as a formal declaration of war, and will not hold itself responsible for the consequences thereof.'

DRAFT OF THE ORIGINAL ULTIMATUM SEPTEMBER 26, 1899

The main points of the actual ultimatum sent to England 9 October 1899:

(a) That all points of mutual difference shall be regulated by the friendly course of arbitration or by whatever amicable way may be agreed upon by this Government with Her majesty's Government.

(b) That the troops on the borders of this Republic shall be instantly withdrawn.

(c) That all reinforcements of troops which have arrived in South Africa since the 1st June, 1899, shall be removed from South Africa within a reasonable time, to be agreed upon with this Government, and with a mutual assurance and guarantee on the part of this Government that no attack upon or hostilities against any portion of the possessions of the British Government shall be made by the Republic during further negotiations within a period of time to be subsequently agreed upon between the Governments and this Government will, on compliance therewith, be prepared to withdraw the armed Burghers of this Republic from the borders.

(d) That Her Majesty's troops which are now on the high seas shall not be landed in any part of South Africa.

This Government must press for an immediate and affirmative answer to these four questions, and earnestly requests Her Majesty's Government to return such an answer before or upon Wednesday the 11th October, not later than 5 o'clock p.m., and it desires further to add that in the event of unexpectedly no satisfactory answer being received by it within that interval it will with great regret be compelled to regard the action of Her Majesty's Government as a formal declaration of war, and will not hold itself responsible for the consequences thereof ...'

LARGELY DRAFTED BY JAN SMUTS BUT SIGNED BY F.W. REITZ: STATE SECRETARY

VC

Edward Brown Major (later Colonel) 14th Hussars: *Gazetted 15 January 1901*

13 Oct 1900: Geluk: Major Brown, seeing that the horse of one of the sergeants had been shot, helped the man up behind him and carried him for about ¾ mile to a place of safety. He did this under heavy fire. Afterwards he helped a Lt to mount his horse which was very restive under heavy fire – the officer could not have mounted without this help. Later, Major Brown carried a wounded lance-corporal out of action to safety.

'WAR IS WAR, AND ALWAYS BAD; BUT SOMETIMES WORSE; FOR THE CAUSE IS STILL A MIGHTY FACTOR, AS THOSE MAY SEE WHO CONTRAST THE PROBABLE EFFECTS UPON THE PEOPLE OF SOUTH AFRICA OF WAR ON THE DRIFTS QUESTION WITH THE ACTUAL RESULTS OF THE JAMESON RAID.' – JPF

'BUT THAT FATAL SURRENDER WAS NOT ONLY THE UNDOING OF OUR BURGHERS; IT ALSO RE-INFORCED THE ENEMY, AND GAVE HIM NEW COURAGE.' – CDW

1900 OCTOBER 2000

1900		2000
Tuesday • **Anniversary of Boer ultimatum to Britain** • **Anniversary of De Wet's crossing of the Vaal into the Transvaal: 1899** • Two repairing parties cut up on railway near Vlakfontein	9	Monday
Wednesday • General Buller prepares to return to England	10	Tuesday
Thursday • Martial law withdrawn from Steynburg and Britstown districts • **Anniversary of the outbreak of war**	11	Wednesday
Friday • French commences his march from Machadodorp to Heidelberg • Indemnity and Special Tribunals Act 1900, promulgated in Cape Colony	12	Thursday
Saturday • One VC • Mahon attacked at Geluk	13	Friday
Sunday *'Again and again the surprise was effected, not by the nation of hunters, but by those rooineks whose want of cunning and veldt-craft had for so long been a subject of derision and merriment.' – CD*	14	Saturday
Monday • Barton's Welshmen and Scottish Yeomanry gain victory and honour in a skirmish with snipers *'The Boers fought for their independence.'*	15	Sunday

'BULLER WOULD FIGHT TO THE DEATH: AND CERTAINLY HE FOUGHT TO THE FURTHEREST POINT POSSIBLE, THAT OF DISMISSAL!'

Talana and Elandslaagte: 1899

Churchill pays tribute to Penn-Symons: referring to the message from a large homeward bound steamer – 'Boers defeated; three battles; Penn-Symons killed'

In that short message eighteen years of heartburnings are healed. The abandoned colonist, the shamed soldier, the 'cowardly Englishmen', the white flag, the 'How about Majuba?', all gone forever. At last, the Boers defeated! Hurrah! Hurrah! Hurrah!

'So Sir Penn Symons is killed! Well, no one would have laid down his life more gladly in such a cause. Twenty years ago the merest chance saved him from the massacre at Isandlwana, and Death promoted him in an afternoon from subaltern to senior captain. Thenceforward his rise was rapid. He commanded the First Division of the Tirah Expeditionary Force among the mountains with prudent skill. His brigades had no misfortunes; his rearguards came safely into camp. In the spring of 1898, when the army lay around Fort Jumrood, looking forward to a fresh campaign, I used often to meet him. Everyone talked of Symons, of his energy, of his jokes, of his enthusiasm. It was Symons who had built a racecourse on the stony plain; who had organised the Jumrood Spring Meeting; who won the principal event himself, to the delight of the private soldier, with whom he was intensely popular; who, moreover, was to be first and foremost if the war with the tribes broke out again; and who was entrusted with much of the negotiations with their jirgas. Dinner with Symons in the mud tower of Jumrood Fort was an experience. The memory of many tales of sport and war remains. At the end the General would drink the old Peninsular toasts: Our men, our women, our religion, our swords, ourselves, sweethearts and wives, and absent friends – one for every night in the week. The night when I dined the toast was "our men". May the State in her necessities find others like him!'

One of the tents was a large marquee for wounded officers, and here I saw General Penn-Symons, the Commander of the English troops. He was mortally wounded and the nurse told me that he could not last out the night. Next morning, as I was again on my way to the camp, I met a bearer-party carrying his body, wrapped in a blanket, and I accompanied them to where they buried him behind the little English chapel.

Deneys Reitz

VC

Alexis Doxat

Lieutenant (later Major) 3rd Battalion: Imperial Yeomanry: *Gazetted 15 Jan 1901*

20 Oct 1900: Near Zeerust: Lieutenant Doxat, with a party of mounted infantry was reconnoitring a position held by 100 Boers on a ridge of kopjes. When the enemy opened a heavy fire on the reconnaissance party they had to retire, but Lieutenant Doxat, seeing that one of his men had lost his horse, galloped back under heavy fire and took him on his own horse to a place of safety.

A WEST-POINTER WITH THE BOERS AT TALANA: COLONEL JOHN BLAKE:

If asked why we didn't capture Colonel Yule and his men as well as all they possessed, I answer that we had no generals. We had only Lucas Meyer and Daniel Erasmus, and the fighting brains of the two together would not suffice to make an efficient corporal.

'ELANDSLAAGTE: A REAL TRIAL OF STRENGTH BETWEEN THE TWO DOMINANT EUROPEAN RACES IN SOUTH AFRICA. WHICH WOULD PREVAIL? WERE THE BRITISH POWER, INFLUENCE AND IDEALS TO PREVAIL IN SA, OR WERE THE KRUGER IDEALS TO EMERGE TRIUMPHANT?'

1900 OCTOBER 2000

1900	Date	2000
Tuesday • Boer attack on Jagersfontein repulsed	**16**	**Monday**
Wednesday • Metheun defeats Tollie de Beer near SchweizerReneke	**17**	**Tuesday**
Thursday • Boers attack Phillippolis • French reaches Ermelo	**18**	**Wednesday**
Friday • Kruger sails from Lorenzo Marques to Marseilles • Boers attack Fauresmith • Hildyard appointed to the command of Natal and South Eastern Transvaal	**19**	**Thursday**
Saturday • One VC • **1st Anniversary: Talana** • De Wet invests Barton at Frederickstad • French occupies Bethal *'A tactical victory but a strategic defeat.' – CD*	**20**	**Friday**
Sunday • **1st Anniversary: Elandslaagte**	**21**	**Saturday**
Monday *'Towns had fallen, both Republics taken over; Kruger had fled and his regime was no more. BUT IT WAS NOT THE END.'*	**22**	**Sunday**

Buller relieved of his command and retired on half pay

23 October 1901

In 1898 that gallant but ill-tempered officer had been appointed to the Aldershot Command for a term of five years. On his departure to South Africa his position had been kept open for him, as was the custom of the service. When he returned just before the end of Wolseley's time, he was allowed to resume his command since, although his record in South Africa had hardly been a brilliant one, he had not done anything to merit actual dismissal. With the formation of the 1st Army Corps at Aldershot, it was decided to let him stay for the two years until his term expired, and until such time as the more successful South African leaders should return. This decision came as a terrible shock to those who had Army reform at heart and caused much adverse comment. At length, goaded by hostile letters to the Press, Buller made a most unfortunate speech at a luncheon given by the Queen's Westminster Volunteers, in which he clumsily answered his detractors even to the point of admitting that he had advised Sir George White to abandon Ladysmith – a telegram which had not been made public by the Government. Since this speech was contrary to every Regulation and the admission it contained revealed its author as quite unfit to hold any position of importance, Roberts first asked him for an explanation. When none was forthcoming Roberts gave him the opportunity of resigning, and then, since he absolutely refused to do so, terminated his appointment.

Buller's cablegram to Wolseley

11.15 p.m. 15 December 1899:

A serious question is raised by my failure to-day. I do not now consider that I am strong enough to relieve Ladysmith. Colenso is a fortress, which, if not captured by a rush could, I think, only be taken by a siege. Within the 8 miles from the point of attack there is no water and in this weather that exhausts Infantry. The place is fully entrenched. I do not think we saw either a gun or a Boer all day, but the fire brought to bear on us was very heavy. The Infantry were willing enough to fight but the intense heat absolutely exhausted them. I consider I ought to let Ladysmith go and to occupy good position for the defence of South Natal and so let time help us. But I feel I ought to consult you on such a step. 20 000 men, I consider, faced us to-day; both in arms and in position they had the advantage. They admit indeed that they suffered severely, but my men are dispirited because they have not seen a dead Boer. My losses have not been very heavy; much heavier indeed I could have made them, but the moment I failed to get on the run the result would have been the same. I was beaten. I now feel that I cannot say that with my available force I can relieve Ladysmith, and suggest that for me to occupy a defensive position and fight it out in a country better suited to our tactics is the best thing I can do.

Buller's heliogram to White after Colenso

16 December 1899:

'I tried Colenso yesterday but failed; the enemy is too strong for my force, except with siege operations, and those will take one full month to prepare. Can you last so long? If not, how many days can you give me in which to take up defensive position? After which I suggest you firing away as much ammunition as you can, and making best terms you can. I can remain here if you have alternative suggestion, but unaided I cannot break in. I find my Infantry cannot fight more than 10 miles from camp, and then only if water can be got, and it is scarce here.'

Churchill on Buller: 'I have no doubt that at his age he no longer possessed the military capacity, or the mental and physical vigour, or the resource and ruthlessness, which his duty required. Nevertheless he continued to command the confidence of his soldiers and remained the idol of the British public. I am doubtful whether the fact that a man who has gained the VC for bravery as a young officer fits him to command an army twenty or thirty years later.'

General Sir Redvers Buller

K.C.M.G., K.C.B., V.C.

Born 1839: entered 60th Rifles, 1858; served in China, 1860; Red River Expedition, 1870; Ashanti War, 1874; Frontier War, 1878; Zulu War, 1878-9; Deputy Adjutant-General, 1885; Under Secretary for Ireland, 1887; Adjutant-General, 1890; Lieutenant-General, 1891; in command at Aldershot, 1898; appointed to command of Army Corps, South Africa, 1899. Sir Redvers Buller arrived in Capetown October 31; having matured his plans he went on to Natal, arriving on November 25.

Colenso: As for General Buller, he gained laurels from his defeat that are not always won by victorious generals. He sacrificed, or let me say, rather, he jeopardised, his own reputation in order to avert an irreparable sacrifice of his army. A weaker man, a less heroic soldier, would have carried the position with an appalling loss of life. Buller's decision to retire was a proof of his bravery and good generalship.

JBA

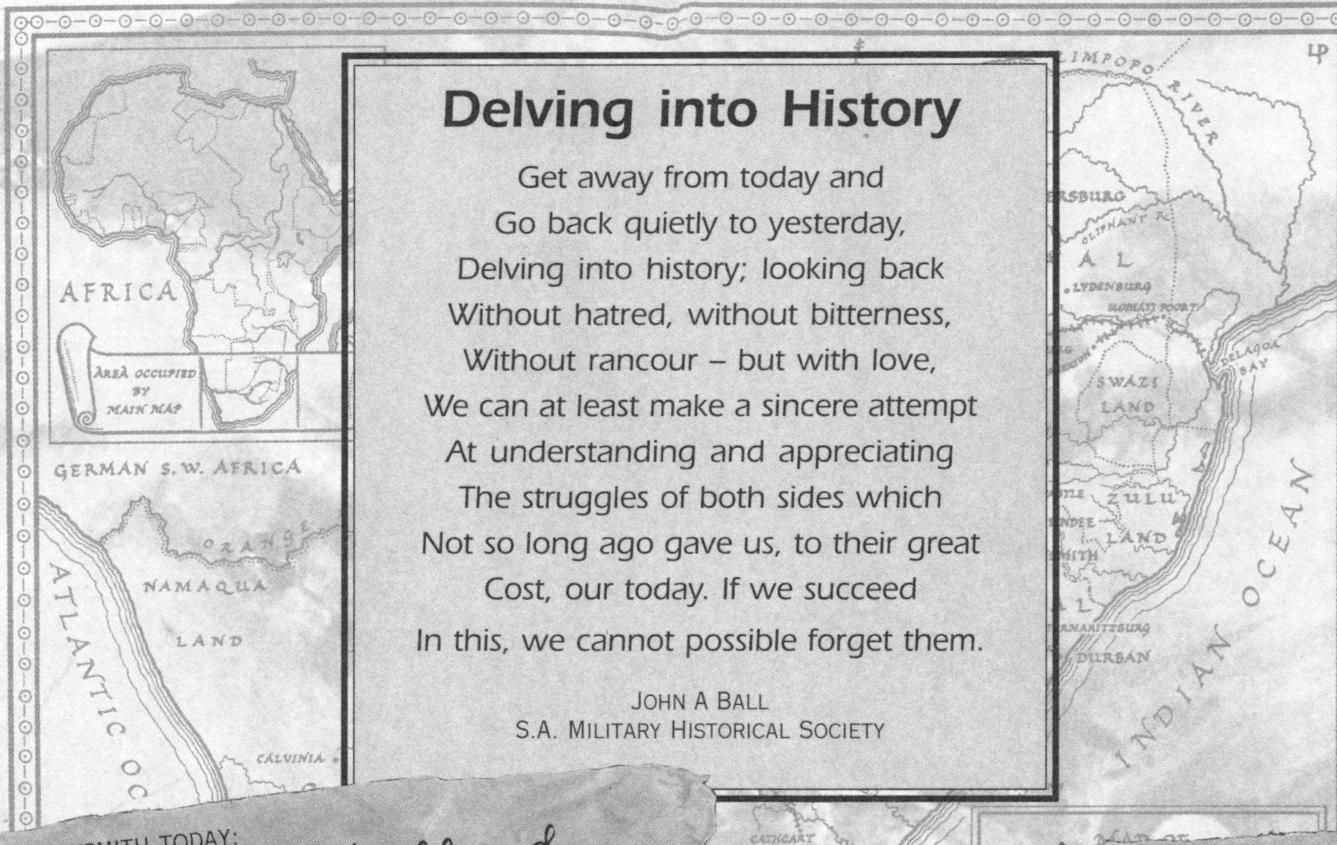

Delving into History

Get away from today and
Go back quietly to yesterday,
Delving into history; looking back
Without hatred, without bitterness,
Without rancour – but with love,
We can at least make a sincere attempt
At understanding and appreciating
The struggles of both sides which
Not so long ago gave us, to their great
Cost, our today. If we succeed
In this, we cannot possible forget them.

JOHN A BALL
S.A. MILITARY HISTORICAL SOCIETY

LADYSMITH TODAY:
Almost every knoll and hill and mountain has a history; almost every acre has received the pressure of besieger and besieged, pursuer and pursued.

'The Royal Engineers were the forerunners of the R.A.F., starting with the 'Balloon Section' (1889 – Aldershot), then the Air Battalion, which later became The Royal Flying Corps, and finally the R.A.F. of today.'

Telecommunication: Both the telephone and telegraph existed in 1899 but their use on the battlefield was limited because commanders did not understand their full potential.

Children's Corner

Tommy's Natural History:

The Boer – This kwaint little creture lives almost intirely on billtong and copies. His body is covered with shells, wich he throus at you wen he's angry, thow it doesn't newer hit you. Nurse says you can find him round Ladysmith any day you like, thow you don't newer see him as he always hides behind rox and fings. He doesn't never throw fings on Sunday, but sits still and redes his prair book, which ma says all good little boys ort to do. He haits pointed fings like bainetts and lances. Pa says he is a woman haiter, but he doesn't hait peticotes as much as kilts. I don't kwite see wot he means, do you? He is such a funny little creture no one older than a seccond leftenant ever underestands wot he'll do next.

1900 OCTOBER 2000

1900		2000
Tuesday *'Time was when in battle after battle a tenth would have been a liberal estimate for the losses of the Boers as compared with those of the Briton. But a year of the kopje and the donga alters all that.'* – CD	**23**	**Monday**
Wednesday • Buller sails from Cape Town for England • Phillippolis relieved • Methuen defeats Lemmer at Kruisrivier	**24**	**Tuesday**
Thursday • Formal proclamation at Pretoria of Annexation of Transvaal • De Wet retires from Frederickstad • Boers attack Jacobsdal	**25**	**Wednesday**
Friday • Koffiefontein repulses Boer attack • French reaches Heidelberg	**26**	**Thursday**
Saturday • Knox captures guns and wagons from De Wet at Rensburg Drift	**27**	**Friday**
Sunday • Methuen and Lemmer engaged at Bronkhorst fontein	**28**	**Saturday**
Monday *'The love and brotherhood among men who have shared great danger is beyond the understanding of women.'* – GANDHI	**29**	**Sunday**

Dum-Dums: A case of the pot calling the kettle black?

Disaster at Nicholson's Nek:

By 29 October 1899, a considerable force of Boers had been located on Long Hill and Pepworth Hill, north of Ladysmith. Parties could even be seen from the outposts preparing emplacements for their 'Long Tom'.

To delay being invested, Sir George White planned to attack the Boers in force and drive them from the hills overlooking the town. A strong detachment was to march 7 miles up the Bell Spruit valley during the night, and occupy a strong position at Nicholson's Nek, behind the Boers' right flank, before dawn on the 30th. This force was given the task of protecting the left flank of the main attack and at the same time of keeping open a way through the hills for the cavalry to dash through, to pursue the enemy when driven from his position and to capture his camps. The 10th Mountain Battery, the 1st Battalion Irish Fusiliers, and the 1st Battalion Gloucestershire Regiment were selected for this dangerous adventure.

The Gloucestershire Regiment paraded at 8.30 p.m. on October 29th, 23 officers and just over 450 men strong, with some 57 of their pack mules carrying a Maxim gun, 90 boxes of reserve S A A, signalling equipment, and one pint of water per man.

The force was to rendezvous on the Newcastle road, just outside the outpost line, at 10 p.m. but was delayed nearly one and a half hours by the late arrival of the Royal Irish Fusiliers, who had paraded with Dum Dum ammunition in their pouches and loaded on their mules, all of which had to be changed to solid S A A, the Home Government having ruled that Dum Dum ammunition was not to be used against the Boers. The delay made it difficult if not impossible for the column to reach its objective before dawn.

The two battalions paraded much under strength, the Royal Irish Fusiliers having to leave one and a half companies behind on outposts and the Gloucestershires two and a half companies. The numbers of the latter were further reduced by many men being laid low with ptomaine poisoning, caused by an issue of tainted cheese.

Based on insufficient information, the end of this ill-conceived operation was the Boers marching nearly the whole of Carleton's column to the railway, and entraining them for Pretoria. On a more positive note, Carleton's column had played its part in saving Ladysmith by detaining a strong force of Boers, said to be over 3 000 strong, for some hours, thus enabling the main body to return and man the defences of the town.

FROM AN EYEWITNESS: LT COL A.H. RADICE, ADJUTANT OF 1ST BATTALION R.I.F. AT NICHOLSON'S NEK

ACCORDING TO LEO AMERY: TIMES HISTORY:

The Glosters and the mountain battery arrived at the rendezvous a little before the appointed hour. Owing to delay in drawing ammunition from the ordnance store, and to considerable difficulty in loading up their ammunition mules, which were newly issued and restive, and which the untrained men did not know how to handle, the Fusiliers did not arrive for an hour after the rest of the column. This delay was destined to have serious consequences.

The Boers were accused of using Dum-Dums … Treacherous 'Veld Peasants'. The fact that the 1st Royal Irish were in Dundee, prior to Nicholson's Nek, leaves a different slant on the matter, especially as they were in fact 'loaded' with them on initial rendezvous the night of 29 October 1899.

MR

BOTH SIDES ON OCCASION USED EXPANDING BULLETS THAT 'MUSHROOMED' INSIDE THE BODY AND LEFT A GAPING WOUND ON EXIT. A LARGE STOCK OF DUM-DUM CARTRIDGES WAS CAPTURED BY THE BOERS AT DUNDEE AND THESE WERE USED IN SUBSEQUENT BATTLES. ORDINARY MAUSER CARTRIDGES WERE ALSO CONVERTED BY SIMPLY CUTTING OFF THE POINT OF THE BULLET. WHOLE BOXES OF BOER AMMUNITION FOUND AT INNISKILLING HILL NEAR LADYSMITH HAD THE TOP CUT OFF TO EXPOSE THE SOFT CORE AND FOUR SLITS SCORED DOWN THE SIDE OF EACH BULLET.

E. HERBERT

According to the Oxford Dictionary: Dum-Dum: a kind of soft-nosed bullet that expands on impact and inflicts laceration. /Dum-Dum in India, where it was first produced/.

Chance of a life-time

I distinctly remember my own impression after the battle of Modder Spruit when General White's 13 000 troops rushed into Ladysmith in disorder. I expected that on the following morning General Joubert would assault the town. One had simply to see that day's fight and the complete demoralisation of the English troops to know that the same men who had driven them off the girdle of kopjes could easily take the unfortified city.

When the next morning came and I saw the Boers quietly smoking their pipes, I thought they were overlooking the opportunity of the war'.

EASTON: NEW YORK JOURNAL

1900	OCTOBER	2000
Tuesday • **1st Anniversary: Mournful Monday** *'The military could commandeer supplies and put non-combatants in well-kept camps.'*	**30**	Monday
Wednesday *'In this last stage of the war the balance is rather in favour of the British, every encounter diminishing the small reserves of Boers rather than the ample forces of their opponents.' – CD*	**31**	Tuesday

The Cry of South Africa

Give back my dead!
They who by kop and fountain
First saw the light upon my rocky breast!
Give back my dead,
The sons who played on me
When childhood's dews still rested on their heads.
Give back my dead
Whom thou hast riven from me
By arms of men loud called from earth's
farthest bound
To wet my bosom with my children's blood!
Give back my dead,
The dead who grew up on me!

OLIVE SCHREINER
9 MAY 1900

'Irreconcilable' becomes First Honorary Colonel

The 2nd Regiment of the ILH in the South African War was commanded by Brigadier-General Sir Duncan McKenzie.

Many famous soldiers, who later won distinction in the First World War, were associated with the regiment during that period. Among them should be mentioned Lieutenant-General Sir Charles Briggs, KCB, KCMG; Major-General Sir G T M Briggs, KCMG, CB, DSO; Major-General Sir Alfred Edwards, KCB, MVO; and Major-General Sir Reginald Barnes, KCB, DSO.

Four VC's were won by members of the regiment, namely Major C H Mullins and Captain Robert Johnstone at Elandslaagte, Trooper Herman Albrecht at Wagon Hill, and Surgeon Captain Thomas Crean at Tyger Kloof.

After the South African War the regiment continued on a volunteer footing until the Act of Union when, in common with other volunteer regiments, it was absorbed in the Union Defence Force.

During the First World War two regiments of the Imperial Light Horse took part in the South-West African campaign. Thereafter most of the members served in France, Italy, the near East, Palestine or East Africa, 150 who had been troopers in South-West Africa gaining commissions.

The regiment went on full-time service in the Second World War on June 10th, 1940, under the command of Lieutenant-Colonel E J R Blake, DSO, ED. With the 1st RDLI and the 1st RLI it made up the 3rd Infantry Brigade under the command of Brigadier C E Borain, DSO, MC, VD, and was attatched to the 2nd South African Division.

Deneys Reitz, the Boer boy who wrote *Commando – A Boer Journal of the Boer War,* son of Francis William Reitz, a former President of the Orange Free State, who, as Secretary of State, signed the Ultimatum, who left the country as an irreconcilable after the conclusion of the Boer War, who chose not to live under the British flag; as Colonel the Honourable Deneys Reitz became the first Honorary Colonel of the Regiment.

Jan Smuts

On Wednesday 1 November 1899 Boer lines of investment drew round Ladysmith

On Thursday 2 November, the last train passed down the railway under the fire of artillery. That night the line was cut about four miles north of Colenso.

Telegraphic communications also ceased.

NEUTRAL CAMP AND HOSPITAL

Established 5 November 1899

Intombi camp: Situated under the shadow of Umbulwana, with 1½miles of railway line running through its +- 2 000 acres; bounded on the South by Intombi Spruit, on the East by the Klip River, on the North by Fourie's Spruit, and on the West by Town Lands bush.

POPULATION 1ST FEBRUARY 1900:

428 Whites; 378 Blacks; 656 Indians = Civilians

Among the civilians the mortality was remarkably small; only 2 whites succumbed to fever, 11 dysentery and diarrhoea and only 9 cases overall of enteric.

FRANCIS REITZ
STATE SECRETARY AND PAST PRESIDENT OFS:
BEFORE LEAVING SA FOR SELF-EXILE:

South Africa

Whatever foreign shores my feet must tread,
My hopes for thee are not yet dead.
Thy freedom's sun may for awhile be set,
But not for ever, God does not forget.

1900 NOVEMBER 2000

1900		2000
Thursday *'By remaining at Ladysmith, the British ensured that the Boers did not get down to Durban and other ports.'*	1	Wednesday
Friday • **Anniversary of final encirclement of Ladysmith: Siege** • Boers attack Smith-Dorrien at Van Wyk's Vlei	2	Thursday
Saturday • Koffiefontein relieved	3	Friday
Sunday • The increased bitterness of the struggle causes much stress and searchings of conscience among some of the people of Great Britain	4	Saturday
Monday • Hunter succeeds Kelly-Kenny in command at Bloemfontein	5	Sunday

VC

Richard Turner
Lieutenant (later Lieutenant-General) Royal Canadian Dragoons: *Gazetted 23 April 1901*
7 November 1900: During the action at Komati River, when the guns were in danger of being captured, Lieutenant Turner, although he had already been twice wounded, dismounted and deployed his men at close quarters and drove off the enemy, thus saving the guns.

VC

Edward Holland
Sergeant (later Lieutenant-Colonel) Royal Canadian Dragoons: *Gazetted 23 April 1901*
7 November 1900: Sergeant Holland kept the Boers away from two 12-pounder guns with his Colt gun. When he saw that the enemy were too near for him to escape with the carriage, as the horse was blown, he calmly lifted the gun off and galloped away with it under his arm.

VC

Hampden Cockburn
Lieutenant (later Major) Royal Canadian Dragoons: *Gazetted 23 April 1901*
7 Nov 1900: During the action at Kamati River, Lieutenant Cockburn with a handful of men, at a most critical moment, held off the enemy to enable the guns to get away. To do so he had to sacrifice himself and his party, all of whom were killed, wounded, or taken prisoner. He himself was slightly wounded.

Boer Hero on Spioenkop:

Commandant Prinsloo

Prinsloo was killed in action later in 1900. He had been slightly wounded in the head during Spioenkop, but resumed command of the Carolina commando after a period in hospital.

He was shot dead in sight of his wife and family 7 November 1900. He had led an attack against a column under General Smith-Dorrien just outside Belfast. He was buried on the field. In 1926 a monument, which owed much to Smith-Dorrien's generosity, was raised to his memory over the grave.

On each anniversary of his death burghers stood gathered in silent tribute to one of the few men who took away from Spioenkop a better reputation than he had brought to it.

NOTES:

1900	NOVEMBER	2000
Tuesday • Defeat of De Wet at Bothaville • Le Gallais killed • The British mounted infantry have reached a point of efficiency at which they are quite able to match the Boers at their own game	**6**	Monday
Wednesday • Three VCs *'If I die, tell my mother that I die happy, as we got the guns.'* – LE GALLAIS	**7**	Tuesday
Thursday • Smith-Dorrien in action at Komati River	**8**	Wednesday
Friday • After the dispersal of the main army at Komatipoort there remained a considerable number of Boers in arms; some irreconcilable burghers; some foreign adventurers and some Cape rebels to whom British arms are less terrible than British law	**9**	Thursday
Saturday • Methuen and Lemmer in action at Wonderfontein	**10**	Friday
Sunday *'Another change in the war lay in those more strenuous measures which the British commanders felt themselves entitled and compelled to adopt.'*	**11**	Saturday
Monday • Irreconcilables, foreigners and rebels spread themselves over the country, and act with such energy that they give the impression of a large force	**12**	Sunday

How an under-esteemed boy of genius
Of noble character and daring spirit
Seized and created a hundred opportunities
To rise in the world
And add glory
By his own merit and audacity
To a name already famous

MARY SOAMES: CHURCHILL'S YOUNGEST DAUGHTER

They all suffered ...

Intercepted letter

The following letter was discovered the other day amongst the bags which were sent back to us, not having succeeded in getting through the Boer lines:

To Mr Smith, Esq., Collector Sahib, Mozuffernugger, NWP India.
November 10, 1899

Most Honoured Sir,
Your humble servant begs to inquire after your egregious and illustrious health. And as above poor petitioner wishes to bring this my humble petition for kind consideration of above. Since after subsequent many days arrival in this place called Lady Smith, undersigned being loyal subject but of timid nature, has suffered cannon balls, and many long toms for these days, and since few days have suffered sickness with pains and spasms.
Sir, I am not a military soldier, and am in constant terror of balls as above. Undersigned would therefore pray that your most noble opulence would bring kind consideration to bear, and bring relief on your honour's most humble and beseeching petitioner, as since many days I am hiding in hole, and dare not make exit from same. Please to give order that I return to your honour's service without delay, for which act of kindness grovelling petitioner will ever pray, as in duty bound, for your honour's long life and prosperity.
Ever your most humble and obedient servant,
Sheo Narain Das,
Baboo.

Mr Oom Paul Kruger, ex-president of the Transvaal, and wandering plenipotentiary of the order of the green sash, has not, it appears, come out of his struggles for right and liberty, for himself and company, without some loss of blood. The Boer blood was drawn in gay Paree. An admirer of the old gentleman threw a bouquet at him with such vigour that it struck his nose, inflicting a scratch, from which blood flowed freely. Who can say after this that Paul has not bled for his country?

1900	NOVEMBER	2000
Tuesday • A large number of farmers break their parole and throw themselves once again into the struggle, adding their honour to the other sacrifices they have made for their country	**13**	Monday
Wednesday • Numerous and continual brushes between scattered bands and British forces make it hard for the writer and intolerable for the reader if they are set forth in detail	**14**	Tuesday
Thursday • **Anniversary of Chieveley train incident and Churchill's capture**	**15**	Wednesday
Friday • Conspirators against Lord Roberts arrested	**16**	Thursday
Saturday • De Wet at the head of a considerable force prepares to attack the British garrison of DeWetsdorp, forty miles south-east of Bloemfontein	**17**	Friday
Sunday • Lord Roberts meets with an accident at Johannesburg • De Wet assails DeWetsdorp	**18**	Saturday
Monday • The Boers fight for their independence: we fight for a shilling a day *'As the months went on and the struggle still continued, the war assumed a harsher aspect, every farmhouse representing a possible fort, and a probable depot for the enemy.' – CD*	**19**	Sunday

Dead men or shattered horses do not give a more vivid impression of the unrelenting brutality of war than the sight of a structure, so graceful and so essential, blown into a huge heap of twisted girders and broken piers.

CD

FIRST PUBLICATION OF LIES: 26 NOVEMBER 1899

The pathetic gratitude with which the first issue of the Ladysmith Lyre was received proves that to appreciate literature of the highest order, you only have to be shut up for a month under shell-fire.

Nevinson

VC

Charles Kennedy

Private: 2nd Battalion: The Highland Light Infantry: *Gazetted 18 October 1901*

22 Nov 1900: Dewetsdorp: Private Kennedy carried a wounded comrade who was bleeding to death, from Gibralter hill to the hospital, a distance of ¾ mile, under very heavy fire. On the following day, he volunteered to carry a message to the commandant across a space over which it was almost certain death to venture.

He did not, however, succeed in delivering the message, as he was severely wounded before he had gone 20 yards.

1900	NOVEMBER	2000
Tuesday • The water supply to the garrison is cut – volunteers bring water at night	**20**	**Monday**
Wednesday • The extended DeWetsdorp position has the fatal weakness in that the loss of any portion means the loss of it all • Thirst in the sultry trenches is terrible	**21**	**Tuesday**
Thursday • One VC • The attack develops at the end of the ridge held by the Highlanders • Every night the Boer riflemen draw closer – every morning finds the position more desperate	**22**	**Wednesday**
Friday • Soldiers hold out all day but thirst is enough to compel surrender • Garrison at Dewetsdorp surrenders to De Wet	**23**	**Thursday**
Saturday • DeWetsdorp falls after a creditable defence • Prisoners gaze with interest at the most famous of the Boer leaders	**24**	**Friday**
Sunday • The extreme measure of burning down farm houses is originally carried out after a definite offence, such as affording cover for snipers	**25**	**Saturday**
Monday • DeWetsdorp re-occupied by General Charles Knox with 1 500 men	**26**	**Sunday**

'MY DEAR GENERAL – MAY WE MEET AGAIN WHEN RIFLES ARE LOADED AND SWORDS SHARPENED – IF POSSIBLE BEFORE AN AUDIENCE WHICH WILL INCLUDE 40 CENTURIES.' – WSCH TO IH

Old Comrades

'Setting the fair sex tenderly but firmly on the mantelpiece, nobody, not even Lord Bobs in all his glory, has touched my life at so many points as Winston Churchill. So much indeed has he done so that were my pages to give no glimpses of his strange voyage through the years, showing him sometimes as the Flying Dutchman, scudding along under bare poles; sometimes as a small boy playing with goldfish; my story would not be complete. As a sample – on the 6th of January '41 Bardia had fallen: – red-hot news. Before it began to cool it must be hammered into all sorts of shapes and handed out through many channels leading to Finance, Parliament and the World. Every second was priceless yet he paused to let his mind fly back forty-one years to send a special message to an old comrade of the wars who had long since ceased to interest Press, Parliament or Finance.'

Post Office Telegram – London 12.54:

GENERAL SIR IAN HAMILTON – BLAIR DRUMMOND – PERTHSHIRE.
I AM THINKING OF YOU AND WAGON HILL WHEN ANOTHER
JANUARY 6TH BRINGS NEWS OF A FINE FEAT OF ARMS.
WINSTON

Winston was several times out with these parties and was not only a real help, but learnt a great deal more about soldiering and the strenuous and dangerous side of war; about dodging bullets, taking up rear-guard positions, and laying ambuscades than he would have learnt by years of parades and polo matches with his own regiment. In fact he learnt exactly what he was to put into practice three years later at Diamond Hill.

Just as the battle of Diamond Hill meant the true turning point of the South African campaign, so the decision I had to make at Gudda Kalai was to be the be or not to be of my own career, now on the point of burying itself in a Scottish graveyard. I.H.

Boer volunteers: The civilian armies of Kruger, many fighting in their Dutch civilian frock-coats, were putting Great Britain to shame and all Europe was laughing at her failures.

BULLER:

Dislikes notoriety, Press or otherwise, and possibly would prefer, like others one wots of, to confine the chronicle of the campaign to official bulletins.'
BB

1900	NOVEMBER	2000
Tuesday • Lord Kitchener succeeds Lord Roberts as Commander-in-Chief • Action at Rhenoster Kop • Roberts succeeds Wolseley as Commander-in-Chief at home	**27**	Monday
Wednesday • De Wet breaks away from Vaalbank and manages to shake off pursuit	**28**	Tuesday
Thursday • Lord Kitchener takes over the command in South Africa	**29**	Wednesday
Friday • Transvaal government reach the Tautesberg • Churchill turns 26	**30**	Thursday

The Ladysmith Pigeon

'In the Natal Archives at Pietermaritzburg there is an extremely interesting map of the country around Ladysmith compiled at military headquarters by the officer-in-charge of the mapping section, Field Intelligence Division, H.C. Simpson. This is a compilation of positions around Ladysmith received from the besieged town itself during November and December 1899.

The fascinating thing about this map is that its details were drawn from information received from 'The Messenger' which was ... a carrier pigeon! So famous was this bird that it was portrayed in "Punch" of November 15, 1899, winging away from Ladysmith with a despatch bag on which is written 'V.R. – O.H.M.S.' Around the pigeon shells are bursting, and underneath there is the Charivarian description: 'The Latest Recruit with the Natal Field Force: Full private pigeon to be mentioned for distinguished conduct as bearer of despatches. Not to be plucked on examination!'

Dr Stark – Ornithologist

Dr Stark: 'A shell came through the roof, glided off a wall, then flying out of the front door, struck Dr Stark, who was standing talking to a friend. The shell severed both his legs and he died in a few hours. He used to live all day in his cave with his favourite cat, carrying the cat about in the day-time in a bag. This fatality happened after some Boer doctors had dined on several occasions at the Hotel. After this the Hotel was closed.'

JANUARY 1915
WINSTON CHURCHILL TO DIRECTOR OF THE AIR DIVISION:

I wish the following experiment made at once: two ordinary steam rollers are to be fastened together side by side, by very strong steel connections, so that they are to all intents and purposes one roller covering a breadth of at least 12-14 feet.

Even in the old days Winston could hardly touch anything or anyone without putting 'go' into them. If it was a tank he poured petrol into it. Others shared with him, no doubt, in the triumph of the tank - several of them put in claims and were duly acclaimed to the tunes of varying wads of bank notes. But Winston had played incomparably the greater part in the material creation and production of that decisive Mother Tank produced at Hatfield Park on the 2nd February 1916. He had pawned his reputation, shouldered grave personal risks and grave financial risks before he could get as far as he did in arranging this crucial demonstration for Lord Kitchener and handing over these super war engines to the army.

Ian Hamilton

In the field, Haig's lack of imagination or even of that sporting boyish instinct which might have replaced it, will show up to the historian of the future a good, laborious, go-by-the-ground Generalissimo making a complete mess of the introduction into his front line of battle of one of the most tremendous military secrets of the ages.

Ian Hamilton

'THE AIR WAS THE FIRST CAUSE THAT TOOK US TO DUNKIRK,
THE ARMOURED CAR WAS THE CHILD OF THE WAR AND THE TANK ITS GRANDCHILD.' – WSCH

Not for them ... the elusive cross

Ian Hamilton and Winston Churchill: friends to the end

There is a Victoria Cross gallantry which leads to nothing save personal decoration, and there is another and far higher gallantry of calculation that springs from a cool brain as well as a hot head and it is from the men who possess this rare quality that great warriors arise.

CD

1900	DECEMBER	2000
Saturday *'It is not too much to say that our weak treatment of the question of horses will come to be recognised as the one great blot upon the conduct of the war.' – CD*	1	Friday
Sunday • De Wet engages Knox at Goed Hoop	2	Saturday
Monday • De la Rey captures convoy at Buffelspoort	3	Sunday

'THEN I MUST MENTION THE PLAGUE OF FLIES. IT WAS ALMOST INCREDIBLE.
THEY PESTERED US BY DAY AND WE COULD NOT KEEP THEM OUT OF OUR FOOD.
AFTER DARK THEY CLUSTERED LIKE A LIVING MAT ON THE CEILING.'

Captain Harry Schofield

Royal Artillery, won his Victoria Cross at the Battle of Colenso during the Boer War on the 15th December 1899. Colonel Long had taken two batteries of Field Artillery and six Naval guns for the main attack. He opened fire on Fort Wylie, a heavily defended Boer position, but had no infantry support and was subject to a withering fire from the outlying trenches. The invisible Boer enemy were expert marksmen and able to pick off the gunners like shooting wild life on their farms, an often repeated situation in the Boer War. The tragedy of Spion Kop comes quickly to mind.

Owing to ammunition running low, the gunners retreated to a donga behind the guns, taking their wounded (including Colonel Long) with them. General Buller wished the guns to be saved and although it was a forlorn hope, Congreave, Schofield and Roberts (Aide-de-Camps to the Generals) rode out assisted by Corporal Nurse. Captain Congreave was wounded, the Hon. Lieutenant Roberts (only son of Lord Roberts) was mortally wounded. Captain Schofield and Corporal Nurse saved two of the guns, Schofield was awarded the D.S.O. and promoted Major. At the time General Buller was of the mind that Schofield was carrying out orders and not showing initiative and therefore did not qualify for the Victoria Cross. But the powers that be soon put this to rights, stating that a Victoria Cross could be gained for deeds performed under orders. The D.S.O. was later changed to the Victoria Cross.

He retired in 1905 and later became a member of His Majesty's Honourable Corps of Gentlemen-at-Arms (1911-1931). During the 1914-18 war he was with the British Remount Commission in Canada and America, afterwards Commandant of Lines of Communication B.E.F., retired Lieutenant.-Colonel 1918.

The helmet was sold to an American at the Autumn Connoisseur Auction 1993 and realised £3,200.

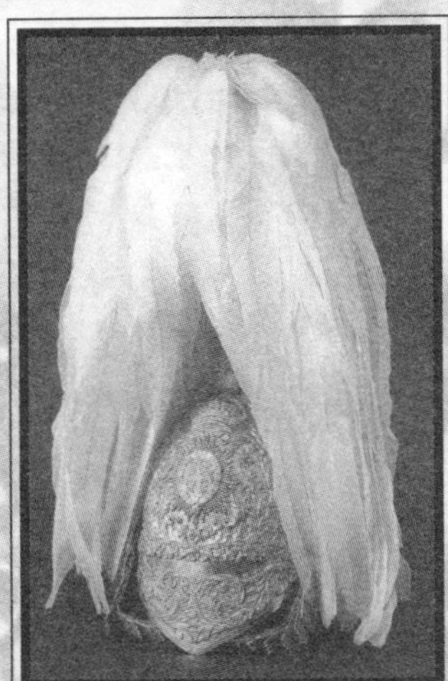

The Gentlemen-at-Arms Helmet worn by Lieutenant-Colonel H.N. Schofield, VC

It was Churchill's South African experience that realised the conception of the tank. – MR

Last of the Gentlemen's Wars

'Finally, whatever may be said of the old Army of 1898-1899, it never lost its sense of chivalry, which is the true dignity of the soldier. However badly it fought, it fought cleanly, and that is a point which should not be forgotten today. It was an army of gentlemen, and elsewhere I have called this war "The Last of the Gentlemen's Wars". It was man against man, and not man against machines (WW1).'

'If the government had listened to Sir Arthur Conan Doyle, who had witnessed first-hand, the horrors of the Boer War, thousands of lives might have been saved in WW1, but the generals took the view that wars were won by throwing as many troops into the battle as possible.'

1900	December	2000
Tuesday *'Our undue and fantastic scruples have prolonged hostilities for months, and cost Britain many lives and many millions of pounds.' – CD*	**4**	Monday
Wednesday • De Wet forced to abandon his projected raid into Cape Colony	**5**	Tuesday
Thursday *'De Wet's plan for the invasion of the Colony cannot be realised, for a tenacious man has set himself to frustrate it.' – Charles Knox*	**6**	Wednesday
Friday • Mr Chamberlain in the House of Commons expounds his policy with regard to the new colonies • Highland Light Infantry post at Commissie Bridge drives off De Wet	**7**	Thursday
Saturday • The Boer leader, realising the game is up, doubles back for safety in the north	**8**	Friday
Sunday • The Boers, still dropping their horses fast, cross the drift at Amsterdam • Knox reaches the Caledon river	**9**	Saturday
Monday • British in touch again near Helvetia in a rearguard skirmish	**10**	Sunday

'Cavalry and infantry were marching to the utmost capacity of men and horses.' – CD

Colonel C J Long, RA

Obtained his Lieutenancy in 1870; served in the Afghan War of 1878-80, and in the Sudan under Lord Kitchener in 1897-8 as Commandant of the Egyptian artillery. He was present at the battle of Khartoum, and for his services on that occasion was mentioned in despatches. Colonel, September, 1899; in command of the Royal Artillery at Colenso, where his anxiety to get within effective range of the enemy led to the loss of ten guns. In that action he was seriously wounded.

Colonel Long, who commanded the artillery at Omdurman, and who has commanded more artillery in action than any British officer, was resolute to see now what he could do with almost no artillery at all.
Colonel Long, as I know, for I travelled from England with him, had a theory, that you must get near to the enemy with your guns
'The only way to smash those beggars is to rush in at them.'

JBA

That damned gunner: On November 15th Colonel Long was in command at Estcourt, and was held responsible for the disaster of the armoured train. I believe he had ordered the officer commanding the train not to go beyond Frere (it was just beyond Frere that the accident happened); but he had given the order verbally, not in writing, for want of time, and so he accepted the responsibility. On the same day of the next month he is held responsible for half the trouble at Colenso. He may be responsible, but he is a good soldier and a gentleman if ever there was one.

JBA

VC

Donald Farmer

Sergeant (later Lieutenant-Colonel) 1st Battalion: The Queen's Own Cameron Highlanders: Gazetted: *12 April 1901*

13 December 1900: During an attack at Nooitgedacht, a Lieutenant with 15 men went to the assistance of a piquet which was heavily engaged, most of the men having been killed or wounded. The enemy immediately opened fire on the relief party, killing two and wounding five, including the Lieutenant. Sergeant Farmer at once went to the officer who was quite helpless, and carried him away under heavy fire to a place of comparative safety, after which he returned to the firing line and was eventually taken prisoner.

VC

William Dick-Cunyngham

Lieutenant (later Lieutenant-Colonel) The Gordon Highlanders: *Gazetted 18 October 1881*

13 December 1879: During the attack on the Sherpur Pass, (Afghan War) there was a momentary wavering of the troops who had been beaten back at the top of the hill. Lieutenant Dick-Cunyngham rushed forward and gallantly exposed himself to the full fire being poured upon this point. He rallied the men by his example and cheering words, and calling on those near to follow him, charged into the middle of the enemy. ***Dick-Cunyngham is buried in Ladysmith Cemetery.***

Dick-Cunyngham: 6 January 1900: Wagon Hill

The day was now dawning, and the whole garrison was thoroughly roused. Four more companies of the Gordons, encamped on the far side of the town, marched out to the fray, headed by their colonel, Dick-Cunyngham. This heroic officer was just expressing his satisfaction at being out of hospital in time for the fray – he had been hard hit at Elandslaagte – and was hurrying his men across the Klip River bridge, when a Boer on the other side of Caesar's Camp fired a Mauser rifle. The bullet missed the target aimed at, skimmed the top of the ridge, flew nearly 3 000 yards (+-2 500m), and smote the colonel of the Gordons. He died soon afterwards.

'POOR DICK-CUNYNGHAM! AFTER ALL YOUR YEARS OF SOLDIERING, AFTER BRAVING DEATH A SCORE OF TIMES, TO BE STRUCK DOWN BY A STRAY BULLET!'

'THE WISE AND RIGHT COURSE, IS TO BEAT DOWN ALL WHO RESIST, EVEN TO THE LAST MAN, BUT NOT TO WITHHOLD FORGIVENESS AND EVEN FRIENDSHIP FROM ANY WHO WISH TO SURRENDER.' – WSCH

1900	December	2000
Tuesday • Both Boer and Brit parties ride through Reddersburg, only a few hours separating them • Lord Roberts sails from Cape Town for England	**11**	Monday
Wednesday • Boer attack at Vryheid repulsed • Sir D. Barbour commissioned to inquire into finances of Transvaal and Orange River Colony	**12**	Tuesday
Thursday • One VC • Clements attacked at Nooitgedacht by De la Rey and Beyers • Kritzinger overwhelms party of Brabant's Horse near Zastron	**13**	Wednesday
Friday • De Wet and Steyn escape through Springkaan's Nek	**14**	Thursday
Saturday • **Anniversary of 1st Colenso** *'Colenso was therefore the first important rung in the ladder that was to carry him only ten years later to the top of his country's affairs.'* – CJB ABOUT LOUIS BOTHA	**15**	Friday
Sunday • **Anniversary of Blood River 1838** • Kritzinger and Hertzog enter Cape Colony	**16**	Saturday
Monday *'I t has been no new feature for native drivers to bolt in a tight corner.'* – BB	**17**	Sunday

'THE COMMANDER OF THE ARTILLERY, COLONEL LONG, WAS ONE OF THOSE DASHING SOLDIERS BRITAIN PRODUCED FROM TIME TO TIME, POSSESSED OF A HIGH DEGREE OF COURAGE AND LITTLE COMMON SENSE.' – JP

Delagoa Bay, then the only harbour in South Africa open to us, was subsequently forbidden us by the Portuguese Government, whose officials even went so far as to arrest eight hundred of our burghers (who, for want of horses, had taken refuge in Portuguese territory), and to send them to Portugal. The ports of German West Africa cannot be counted among those which were available for us. Not only were they too far from us to be of any service, but also, in order to reach them, it would have been necessary to go through English territory, for they were separated from us by Griqualand West, Bechuanaland, and isolated portions of Cape Colony. We had, therefore, during the latter portion of the war, to depend for supplies upon what little we were able to capture from the enemy.

CdW

'If I were a Boer I hope I should be fighting in the field'

'Churchill's magnanimity towards his former foes won him many friends among the Boers; friends such as Louis Botha and Jan Smuts, who were to prove firm allies during the two World Wars.'

BR

The last VC of the war was also one of the most remarkable. It was awarded to the first man in history to win the cross twice: Lieutenant Martin-Leake, RAMC: 8 February 1902: Vlakfontein, and 29 October 1914: near Zonnebeke: Belgium.

Seventy-eight VCs were won by troops under British command, including detachments from Australia, New Zealand and Canada - the 'cubs', as contemporary posters rather coyly put it, 'coming to the mother lion's call'.

1900	December	2000
Tuesday *'The Boers are difficult to coax to close quarters.'* *– BB*	**18**	**Monday**
Wednesday • Hertzog occupies Phillipstown • Boer raid into Cape Colony	**19**	**Tuesday**
Thursday • Martial law proclaimed in northern Cape Colony	**20**	**Wednesday**
Friday • Meeting of the Burgher Peace Committee in Pretoria	**21**	**Thursday**
Saturday • Reinforcements ordered out to South Africa • Boer movement in Cape Colony checked	**22**	**Friday**
Sunday • Judge Hertzog of the Free State commands about 1 200 well-mounted horsemen; with him is Brand, the son of the former president	**23**	**Saturday**
Monday • Kitchener arrives at Naauwpoort to organize expulsion of the Boers from Cape Colony	**24**	**Sunday**

The Baby's Name …

The War, the War, the bloomin' War,
Has drove my wife insane,
From Kruger to Majuba,
She's had Transvaal on the brain:
And when to christen our first child
Last Sunday week we tried,
The parson cried
'What's this child's name?'
And my old girl replied …

The baby's name is Kitchener,
Carrington, Methuen, Kekewich,
White,
Cronje, Plumer, Powell, Majuba,
Gatacre, Warren, Colenso, Kruger,
Capetown, Mafeking, French,
Kimberley, Ladysmith, Bobs,
Union Jack, Fighting Mac,
Lyddite, Pretoria BLOBBS!

The parson said: 'I can't such names
Upon an infant pop',
My wife she broke his rolling veldt
And smashed his Spion Kop!
She jumped upon his Runsted
And she never made a miss.
She said, 'I'll bust your armoured
train
If you can't remember this.'

The baby's name is Kitchener,
Carrington, Methuen, Kekewich,
White,
Cronje, Plumer, Powell, Majuba,
Gatacre, Warren, Colenso, Kruger,
Capetown, Mafeking, French,
Kimberley, Ladysmith, Bobs,
Union Jack, Fighting Mac,
Lyddite, Pretoria BLOBBS!

Sister Charleson

INTOMBI HOSPITAL CAMP: CHRISTMAS 1899:

'We were put on half-rations before Christmas. The quantity of tinned milk was rapidly decreasing and as cows' milk had been at all times scarce, we began to feel badly off for feeding the sick. We ourselves had not had milk for many weeks.

Christmas Day dawned, but with it no pleasurable feelings. I was thankful that I had no patients on full diet, for I had no extra dainty to give them. Sir George White most kindly sent us sisters a gift of some groceries. Our mess orderly tried to make us a plum pudding, but it was a great failure, for there was no fat or suet in it. On the whole, Christmas Day was very disappointing. Our faith in our soldiers alone kept us from despair, for we felt if we could wait patiently and suffer sickness and hunger our garrison would never surrender, and the day must come when we should be free once more.'

Africa was the launching ground for Churchill's momentous career. It could have started anywhere, but it was South Africa that happened to provide him with his first break. His previous experiences – in Cuba and in India – demonstrated his determination to carve a name for himself; in South Africa he succeeded.

BR

WW1: The total weight of all the shells fired in South Africa during the Boer War was fired in one barrage – in exactly 35 minutes in the Great War. The shelling never ended.

J. ORFORD:
SA MILITARY HISTORY JOURNAL

1900	**December**	**2000**
Tuesday • Action at Rhenoster Kop • Hertzog's column heads into the Cape Colony, apparently for Fraserburg and Beaufort West	**25**	Monday
Wednesday • Action at South Rand Mine, near Greylingstad • General Charles Knox engages De Wet near Leeuw Kop	**26**	Tuesday
Thursday • Martial law extended to Beaufort West and Carnarvon	**27**	Wednesday
Friday • De Wet, frustrated in his attempts to break through to the south, withdraws to Senekal • Cape raiders driven northward	**28**	Thursday
Saturday • Capture of Helvitia post	**29**	Friday
Sunday • Preparations made for the frustration of a more ambitious Boer raid into Cape Colony	**30**	Saturday
Monday *FORAGE: 'We are again without food for our horses, and there is none to be had for love or money. Grazing is nil, and as we have had two days of this now, we'll soon have to go on a foraging expedition to see what we can find.'*	**31**	Sunday

1901 TOWARDS 2001 AD 2001

The fault lay not altogether with the generals. The lack of adequate preparation, of organised information, the terrible immobility of their forces hampered them at every turn.

–Leo Amery

The lesson both of the South African and of the American Civil War is that the light Horseman who is trained to fight on foot is the type of the future.

Conan Doyle

Concluding thought:
Defining history:
The never-ending repetition of the wrong way of doing things.

Gerald Durrell

As for the British the war had taken them unprepared. They started behind-hand and they never made up what they had lost. The scheme on which all their calculations were framed was unstrategical in its character, and based on an unwarrantable underestimate of the enemy's fighting capacity.

IN RETROSPECT: AFTER SPIOENKOP

Had the British Army possessed its Botha, what might it not have achieved, asked even the plain burghers. And the time was coming when the British Army should find a Botha – and a greater than Botha – a general who had skill to plan, faith to inspire, and capacity unflinchingly to execute.

HWW

Louis Botha